M000249681

It's Not Rocket Science:
A Guide to the School Improvement Cycle

"Rich with examples, focused on goal-directed implementation and refinement, and asks for developing a theory of action and improvement. This rocket hits the target."

John Hattie, Emeritus Laureate Professor

"This book provides a practical and evidence-based response to the challenge that while we know improvement cycles work, we are also aware of the difficulties of making them business-as-usual. Misinterpretations, misunderstanding and confusion can hinder our resolve to 'get better at getting better.' The outline of common 'failure points' such as the failure to link teacher learning to student outcomes is helpful; from there, the book focuses on processes and practices that can make ongoing school improvement efficient, non-intrusive and core to all we do (not an extra). I particularly like the explanation of various analysis tools such as the Fishbone, Driver, and Impact v. Ease diagrams. While the book acknowledges that there is rarely a single factor leading to any given concern, it also brings a simplicity to improvement efforts by 'cutting through' to the practices that make a difference. In doing so, it is respectful of the work of leaders, middle leaders, teachers and broader school communities. The WHY of this work resounds clearly: great educational outcomes for our students."

Carmel Kriz, Assistant Director: Teaching and Learning
Catholic Education, Diocese of Rockhampton
Queensland, Australia

"At last! A useful text that draws on our own schooling context to provide much needed clarity and guidance about 'what counts' as an improvement cycle. This book weaves theory and practice together, in ways that provide practical insight to the sequence of improvement cycles. I particularly appreciated the time spent addressing common ways 'improvement cycles' can be misinterpreted and enacted in schools, wasting precious time and energy. This book is 'a must have' for anyone who wants to do the real work of school improvement in ways that will make a positive difference for students and teachers."

Dr Anne S. Hynds, Senior Researcher, Ihi Research
Wellington, New Zealand

"Having worked with Linda and Frauke on improvement in my own school I know that they are not just speaking about theory here but from experience of what actually works in schools. It may not be rocket science but sometimes you need a book like this to focus on what is important and remove the clutter of everyday distractions in school. I have found that if you are able to focus on a clear action plan for improvement then these improvements do come - you then gain clarity on the important things to focus on."

Tom Webb, Principal, Mangere College,
Auckland, New Zealand

"Bendikson and Meyer's book unravels the mystery of the often-misunderstood concept of school improvement. Drawing on their research and successful experience in supporting schools, Linda and Frauke provide achievable, practical steps that help school leaders drive improvement. Applying their user-friendly School Improvement Cycle, the authors show schools how to become intentionally sharp in their daily work. With practiced application, Bendikson and Meyer's insights will transform school improvement and become anchored in the heart of a school's culture. An excellent resource for leaders who strive for continuous improvement in their schools."

Anne Duncan, Workstream Lead, and Kevin Williams,
Deputy Workstream Lead, Capability and Enablement of Our People,
Catholic Schools Broken Bay, Sydney, Australia

"What a breath of fresh air!
It's Not Rocket Science: A Guide to the School Improvement Cycle by Linda Bendikson and Frauke Meyer offers school leaders a uniquely practical insight into a set of research-informed principles and easily applied strategies for leading successful school improvement.
As they reflect on the research-informed insights provided throughout the book, everyday leaders in everyday schools will discover that leading improvement is not a mystical undertaking after all. *It's Not Rocket Science* skillfully combines relevant and up-to-date research with clear insights and pragmatic approaches, resulting in a step-by-step model of school improvement which is further enriched and informed by relevant case studies.
It's Not Rocket Science is a book that schools leaders at all career stages will find informative, accessible and above all else, useful! Get it, apply it. . . transform your school's leadership!"

Richard Newton, Senior Leadership Consultant,
Tui Tuia Learning Circle, University of Auckland

"The Swedish Education Act states that school principals should systematically pursue equitable results, through data collection of student outcomes among other things. Administrative tasks and the requirement for documentation risk taking time away from the school's main mission; that the students should acquire and develop knowledge. My experience as a former Head of School is that many schools struggle with abstract and overarching goals that sometimes lack the student perspective, and without first having thought about how to measure knowledge development. The school leader needs to create conditions (time and tools) throughout the school year, to follow up and reflect on the process of goals and activities always from the student's perspective. This is what *It's Not Rocket Science* delivers: guidance on how to do this."

Vera Sandin, Education Consultant, Stockholm, Sweden

"As a professor of educational leadership in Norway, I have had the great pleasure of reading this book. This is a very down-to-earth and practical book with models and tools that will be very useful for all school leaders, not just in New Zealand, Australia and the Pacific Island nations but also in the rest of the world. The book gives us a reminder that school development is an ongoing process. It is a book I can recommend for school leaders who want support in their pursuit of improvement."

Professor Anne Berit Emstad, Innovation Leader
Department of Teacher Education, Faculty of Social and Educational
Sciences, Norwegian University of Science and Technology

"The aim of the authors was 'to make the complex work of improving student learning and outcomes, at least, somewhat simpler'. In my view, they have succeeded in this goal!

In my 'practitioner-researcher' role I have facilitated innumerable development projects and appraised 112 principals. I have always exhorted the employment of a collaborative action research based, cyclical, approach to development and improvement. The 'School Improvement Cycle' model outlined in this book deeply aligns with several elements of an action research approach and, as such, helps leaders in schools to provide depth and structure when grappling with problems and enacting improvement and change.

It's Not Rocket Science is a highly practical book, designed to both provide step by step guidance and practical examples of application in schools. The strength of the book lies in the way that the latter examples as case studies are used in subsequent chapters to illustrate each step of the School Improvement Cycle model. Detailed descriptions are provided (particularly the inclusion of clear evidence of specific outcomes) for each step in a way that is often missing in many books associated with improvement models. The use of very specific examples of employment of data from the case studies in decision making points in the model is a highlight.

The importance of authentic, genuinely inclusive, collaboration at each step in the model is included in Chapter 11. In my experience even the best laid steps in a plan/model, quickly fold without such significant collaboration and subsequent ownership of change. This topic is worthy of an accompanying book on its own and I encourage the authors to consider that."

Professor Eileen Piggot-Irvine
Auckland University of Technology, New Zealand
Adjunct Professor, Royal Roads University, Canada

"More than a leadership text for individual stakeholders, *It's Not Rocket Science* provides an opportunity for teams to apply a sequence of practical strategies enabling sustainable student achievement and transformation. In times of uncertainty and competing agendas, this coherence-maker promotes teachers as leaders and collaborators, focussing on precise, bite-sized achievable steps that lead to goal achievement and school progress. The 'self-propelling' methodology outlined in this book promotes a culture of internal commitment and inclusion, drawing everyone into the plan with role clarity and expectation. Schools often have a high impact on individual students and cohorts, however, it is the whole school collective efficacy required for sustainable success that this book will ensure."

Tim Hardy, Head of Leading and Learning,
Catholic Education Parramatta Diocese
New South Wales, Australia

It's Not
Rocket Science

It's Not Rocket Science

A Guide to the School Improvement Cycle

BY Linda Bendikson
and Frauke Meyer

Myers
Education
Press

Gorham, Maine

Myers Education Press is an academic publisher specializing in books, e-books, and digital content in the field of education. All of our books are subjected to a rigorous peer review process and produced in compliance with the standards of the Council on Library and Information Resources.

Library of Congress Cataloging-in-Publication Data available from Library of Congress.

13-digit ISBN 978-1-9755-0542-4 (paperback)
13-digit ISBN 978-1-9755-0543-1 (library networkable e-edition)
13-digit ISBN 978-1-9755-0544-8 (consumer e-edition)

Printed in the United States of America.

All first editions printed on acid-free paper that meets the American National Standards Institute Z39-48 standard.

Books published by Myers Education Press may be purchased at special quantity discount rates for groups, workshops, training organizations, and classroom usage. Please call our customer service department at 1-800-232-0223 for details.

Cover design by Michael De Young. Artwork is by Paul Judd based on a painting "What Happened Anyway".

Visit us on the web at **www.myersedpress.com** to browse our complete list of titles.

CONTENTS

DEDICATION

Linda's dedication:
For 'my man', Pav, (1950-2016)
and for my dad, Carl, (1928-2022).

Frauke's dedication:
For my mother, Vera, (1950-2008)
and for my grandmother, Rosemarie, (1919-2018).

LIST OF FIGURES AND TABLES

Figures

Tables

ACKNOWLEDGMENTS

This book owes its practical relevance to the many schools and their leadership teams that have worked with us over the past 10 years. Some schools we have worked with feature prominently in the book under pseudonyms in case studies, and others feature by way of the measurement tools that they developed and allowed us to share in the book, or by the contributions to our understanding of school improvement they made more generally. A special thank you goes to Catholic Schools Broken Bay (CSBB) and the Catholic Education Diocese of Parramatta (CEDP) for the opportunity to work in depth with so many of their schools. Schools featured in this book include, but are not limited to, the following:

Auckland Girls' Grammar School, Auckland, New Zealand
Bucklands Beach Primary School, Auckland, New Zealand
Corpus Christi Catholic Primary School, St Ives, CSBB, Sydney, Australia
Glenview Primary School, Hamilton, New Zealand
Mary MacKillop Catholic Primary School, CEDP, Sydney, Australia
Mangere College, Auckland, New Zealand
Melville High School, Hamilton, New Zealand
One Tree Hill College, Auckland, New Zealand
Our Lady of the Rosary St Mary's Catholic Primary School, CEDP, Sydney, Australia
Sacred Heart Catholic Primary School, Mt Druitt, CEDP, Sydney, Australia
St Bernard's Catholic Primary School, Berowra, CSBB, Sydney, Australia
St Cecilia's Catholic Primary School, Wyong, CSBB, Sydney, Australia
St Mary's Catholic Primary School, Rydalmere, CEDP, Sydney, Australia
St Patrick's Catholic Primary School, Asquith, CSBB, Sydney, Australia
St Paul's Catholic College, Manly, CSBB, Sydney, Australia
And the many other schools we have worked with in Australia, New Zealand, and the Pacific Islands.

Linda and Frauke

FOREWORD

This book has a provocative title: *It's Not Rocket Science - A Guide to the School Improvement Cycle*. Our current reality, however, indicates that it is harder to improve schools than to launch rockets. Not nearly as many failed rockets litter the planet as failed school improvement efforts.

Linda Bendikson and Frauke Meyer use their work in schools to break down the complexity of schooling improvement and provide a step-by-step improvement cycle to guide school leaders in unpacking what is involved in becoming more successful. One hopes that the litter of failed improvement efforts will be removed from the education landscape at the same time.

The authors also present strong challenges to leaders who, if they want to take the work of schooling improvement seriously, need to keep focused on it, create effective internal systems and routines, and reject inadequate teaching. Maybe this is why so many improvement efforts fail. Schools find it so difficult to de-clutter and deal adequately with distractions, along with ensuring that every teacher is teaching as competently as they are able. These challenges for individual schools mirror those of most education systems that create the busy work of distractions and treat schooling improvement as an optional extra rather than the core business of every school.

The authors refer to the importance of planning the early steps. The concept of this kind of planning may be very different from the way many educators think of planning—such as developing an annual action plan. Given the complexity of educational settings, it is not possible to plan how things will develop over a year, because the unexpected always happens. Rather, intensive planning needs to take place near the beginning of the improvement cycle, with subsequent planning being responsive to the outcomes that emerge. As the authors suggest, improvement cycles are rapid tests of ideas that are actioned and responded to, with new plans emerging in light of what is revealed and the success or lack thereof of their improvement efforts.

Responsive adjustments through iterative improvement cycles involve more than adjusting actions. As leaders and teachers learn more deeply through the improvement cycles, they learn how to adjust their measurements to provide more relevant and accurate information, revise their theories for improvement to make them more targeted, and rethink their causal assumptions. Professional learning rarely addresses these important issues; however, they are fundamental to the success of professional learning within the schooling improvement context.

Each stage of the improvement cycle is both described in detail and illustrated through case studies that bring the improvement cycle to life. The authors do not shy away from the challenges involved. It may not be rocket science, but it is not easy. It is made challenging mainly through embedded practices in education systems and the schools within them, which often distract and disrupt those involved from maintaining a narrow focus on student outcomes until they improve and find rigorous monitoring counter to accepted cultural practices. Persistence cannot be timebound, with the next priority already identified before the impact of the current one is assessed. Persistence means continuing with that narrow focus until targeted student outcomes improve. This is the human side of leading improvement that provides the greatest challenges.

Are we more successful in launching rockets than in improving schools, because once the systems are in place, technology takes precedence, and feedback from failure is instantaneous? I suggest that the failure of a school to educate many of our most vulnerable students and adequately address equity issues is likely to have far greater societal consequences than launching a particular rocket.

Helen Timperley, PhD
Professor Emeritus of Education
University of Auckland
New Zealand

INTRODUCTION

This book provides a step-by-step guide for principals, senior leaders, middle leaders, and system leaders to implement improvement cycles in schools. This edition is aimed at New Zealand, Australia, and Pacific Island nations in particular, because the examples within the book are based on the real experiences of Australasian schools. Nonetheless, we believe that a school leader in any country will be able to understand and connect with the examples and make links to their own contexts.

We aim to make the complex work of improving student outcomes, at least, somewhat simpler. We draw on a range of evidence from international research and our own research and development work in schools to describe and illustrate improvement steps that we have found to work in practice and provide examples to show the application of these ideas. If implemented properly, improvement cycles become "self-propelling", and reduce the cognitive load involved in planning how to improve.

We entitled the book "It's not rocket science" because that is what we commonly hear once leaders understand improvement cycles. Once leaders have successfully engaged with the cycles and enacted them a few times, they think: "This is really quite straightforward", and they keep working this way because they see the rapid improvement in student outcomes. However, it is only straightforward if there is good insight into the nature and importance of some of the early planning steps of the cycle. Those steps lay the foundation for success. This work can look messy for the uninitiated or for those undertaking their first cycles; thus, in this book, we walk leaders through these steps with practical guidance and exemplars.

We know from our research and years of interaction with schools that, despite the promotion of improvement cycles by authorities, school leaders are rarely successful in using them to consistently improve outcomes. Some see using improvement cycles as an "extra", or just another project. It is not. It is a way of leading strategically in schools and, indeed, in any organisation. Some think that cycles are something that take a year to proceed through. They are not. Cycles are meant to be rapid "tests" of improvement ideas that drive systemic improvement. Innovations that are successful are then integrated into systems and routines and become "business-as-usual".

We want to help educational leaders to do their job more efficiently. Leaders set the conditions that enable teachers to teach effectively. It is the leaders who are responsible for the results. If they are not getting the results they desire, this is ultimately their problem. If teachers are not teaching well, it is because leaders allowed that to happen. If the school is not resourced adequately, it is because leaders failed to prioritise resources effectively. It is the leaders' job to set a clear improvement agenda and to manage the organisation well by creating good systems and routines. That is the core role of educational leadership, and it can be fulfilled by leading through improvement cycles.

What Are We Building On?

Our School Improvement Cycle builds on research and other models of improvement cycles that have been used in business, health, and education. There were various efforts to solve problems and improve quality by different individuals and organisations in the late 19th and early 20th centuries, including Frederick Winslow Taylor and John Dewey. The work of Mayo and Hawthorn in Western Electric's factory in the 1920s and early 1930s is also cited as early work on improvement methodologies (e.g., King & Kovacs, 2015). But the genesis of improvement cycles is usually credited to Dr Walter Shewhart, who invented an improvement cycle in 1939 to enhance the production of goods (Moen & Norman, 2010). He turned the (initially) linear process of *specification*, *production*, and *inspection* of goods into a cycle with the *inspection* informing improvements for the next cycle (Moen & Norman, 2010).

Nevertheless, the similarities to the work of social psychologist Kurt Lewin in the 1940s are very strong. He proposed the concept of *action research*, which followed a very similar cycle of planning, action, and fact-finding to address social issues. Later action research models are described as iterative cycles of *plan, act, observe,* and *reflect* in order to address context-specific problems (e.g., Cardno & Piggot-Irvine, 1996; Piggot-Irvine, 2009). These steps are repeated at varying stages of the action research process: at the reconnaissance stage, where the research question is investigated and analysed, and at the implementation and evaluation phases. These cycles are depicted as a spiral with one cycle leading to the next, and sometimes with "spin-off" cycles of investigation. Like improvement cycles, action research is intended as a collaborative inquiry for improvement that focuses on evidence-based decision making, hence providing practitioners with a model to use theory in practice and develop theory from their practice.

But it is Walter Shewhart's student, Deming, who brought the idea of an improvement cycle to Japan to support that country's industry in its recovery effort after World War II, and from there, this model gained traction in business settings. Deming built on Shewhart's work by adding a fourth step and called his cycle the "Deming Wheel" (see Figure 0.1). The four steps were: (1) designing and testing a product in-house; (2) making it; (3) marketing it; and (4) testing it in service. This latter step would now be called "market research" and leads to tweaks in the product, or re-design, in light of consumer feedback. This simple approach was so successful that Japan soon became the standard setter in producing high-quality goods for a reasonable price, and the idea of improvement cycles spread in the business world.

The improvement cycle has seen different revisions and modifications since the initial Deming Wheel. However, the main steps remain similar. For example, the Japanese redefined the Deming Wheel as the *Plan-Do-Check-Act (PDCA)* cycle, which was more explicit about the need to determine goals and targets, and methods for reaching them (Moen & Norman, 2010). Their sales figures and customer feedback were their "check" on product quality. If the results were not satisfactory, they returned to the *planning* step; but if the results were satisfactory, they standardised the solution. In the educational version of a cycle, we use short-term measures to check the effectiveness of our teaching or organisational strategies, and then revise them if we do not see improvement. As in industry, we make our solution a

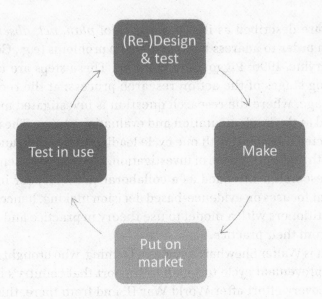

Figure 0.1. The Deming Wheel

new routine if it is effective. The Japanese also instituted the use of basic tools as part of the improvement process, including checklists, fishbone diagrams, and specific graphs and charts to map the process or the results of tests. These are still used as core tools in improvement cycles today, and some will be introduced in later chapters.

Deming claimed that the PDCA was very different from his wheel but, by the 1980s, he promoted the very similar *Plan-Do-Study-Act* (*PDSA*) cycle. The difference between the Japanese step of "checking" and Deming's "studying" seems trivial, but Deming emphasised the importance of comparing results to the predictions made at the planning stage, and formally summarising learning before moving to further action. He argued that checking alone was not enough. Further iterations of the improvement cycle saw more details added to specific steps. For example, by the 1990s, Deming's colleagues Moen, Nolan, and Provost added clarifying questions at the *Plan* stage (Moen & Norman, 2010) to ensure a specific goal was set, a short-term measurement tool was created, and actions defined.

More recently, Langley and colleagues' (2009) book on the improvement cycle re-introduced the notion of the early *Design and test* step that had disappeared with the transition from the Deming Wheel to the PDSA cycle. This step was meant to ensure that the improvement strategy was tested before its wider implementation. Langley and colleagues emphasised that improvement was not achieved by implementing one cycle, but through a series of cycles of testing and re-testing (see Figure 0.2). This series of cycles shows that the improvement process involves a small test of the measures and improvement strategies in one context to start (e.g., in one classroom), and then expands the testing to other contexts (e.g., more classrooms, or a department), before scaling up and embedding it in a wider context (e.g., the whole school). Through the first cycle, the effectiveness of the improvement strategy is tested, but the measurement tool is also tested to establish whether it provides enough and the right kind of data.

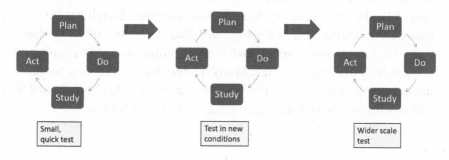

Figure 0.2. Iterative Cycles Based on Figure 7.2 in Langley et al., 2009

Improvement cycles have seen a wide uptake in business and public health (e.g., Gawande, 2011; Langley et al., 2009) but also in the education sector in the late 20th and early 21st centuries (e.g., Bryk et al., 2015; Tichnor-Wagner et al., 2017). Improvement cycles in education have mainly drawn on the *Plan-Do-Study-Act* cycle set out by Deming or the revised version by Langley. Bryk and colleagues (2010) are perhaps best known for their work in school improvement, particularly in large reform efforts.

The *Spiral of Inquiry, Learning, and Action* (Timperley et al., 2014) is a well-known cycle that was designed specifically with schools in mind. The Spiral differs from other improvement cycles by clarifying a first step of scanning a wide range of data before narrowing to a goal focus. It is also overt about the need for users to create hunches (theories) about the causes of the problem to design responses. Finally, it specifically mentions the *learning* required to solve any problem, a step not typically mentioned in cycles. The Spiral involves six stages: (1) scanning; (2) focusing; (3) developing a hunch; (4) learning; (5) taking action; and (6) checking.

In examining the different iterations of the improvement cycle, it becomes evident that the core ideas tend to remain the same but with different emphases added. Further, there is a lot of evidence that improvement cycles work, and their implementation can achieve results, but there is also evidence of the challenge of creating a culture where using cycles is "business-as-usual" (Tichnor-Wagner et al., 2017). In our work, we have frequently witnessed the misinterpretation of the improvement cycle and particularly of the education-specific *Spiral of Inquiry, Learning, and Action*. All too often we have witnessed confused leaders misunderstanding and mis-managing the implementation of cycles. Many leaders have confessed to never having completed a cycle, despite starting many. This book hopes to address this confusion and numerous misinterpretations.

What Problems Do We Hope to Address?

In our research and development work, we have noticed at least five key problems in the way improvement cycles are interpreted and enacted. We outline them below and note how our School Improvement Cycle and this book aim to address these problems.

Time Spent Planning

We see schools taking up to 10 weeks every year stuck in the planning step before starting to focus on testing their theories, and they repeat this pattern year after year. While deep analysis is important, all too often school teams get lost in the data and lose focus at the early planning stage. They frequently do not know what data to focus on, or how to manage the information and discern what data are most important. Cycles of improvement are supposed to be rapid, and the first cycle that one undertakes will necessarily be more challenging and take longer to plan than subsequent cycles because of the need to develop and test measurement tools and initial theories. However, the planning stage should not be overly extended; if it is, the team will lose motivation and focus. The cycles are self-driving, as each cycle inevitably leads to further inquiry into why schools are getting unsatisfactory results. This inquiry leads to some *re-design* of strategies, and schools proceed around the cycle again. So, after the first cycle, planning should not take an extended amount of time.

Failure to Form a Clear Goal

Many schools fail in the planning or the focusing stage of the spiral, where they are supposed to clarify a goal focus and narrow it down to an attainable step. For instance, we often find schools approach the goal-setting stage with unclear goals and load them with assumed solution strategies. Here is one recent example: "Improve student learning through culturally responsive practices". This goal is problematic for two reasons. First, the goal does not point to specific learning outcomes that are desired for students. What aspect of student learning does the school want to improve? In our view, the focus to improve should be on a specific student-learning outcome. Second, the goal assumes that the solution is to focus on "culturally responsive practices". The specific problem to be solved remains unclear, but they have already jumped ahead to an assumed solution. Setting out with an assumed solution will hinder leaders from keeping an open mind when they come to the causal analysis and strategy-design step. Thus, embedding one proposed solution in the goal is not helpful in guiding an improvement cycle. This is a typical approach to problem-solving in schools. As noted by Mintrop and Zumpe (2019), "solutions may be looking for problems they might fight" (p. 300), or, as we describe it, school leaders frequently have "a solution in search of a problem".

Failure to Create Short-Term Outcomes and Measures

Most schools, in our experience, fail to define how they will measure improvement in relation to outcome data or implementation of strategies (process data) before they act. Without a short-term measure, they lack baseline data on student outcomes, or on teacher or leader actions. Hence, they do not know where they started and therefore do not know how much progress they have made at the completion of a cycle. Whether progress is being made might only be evident at the end of the year when they collect summative data, but then it is too late to address the problem. The steps of designing and testing a short-term measure and establishing a baseline are not explicitly stated in most improvement cycles and are commonly missed.

Failure to Link Adult Learning with Student Outcomes

The professional learning undertaken by schools implementing cycles often does not address the causes of the problem, because the professional learning is not directly connected to student outcomes. To be effective, a school has to put in place the changes they think will address the causes of the problem and, as a result, lead to improvement. Then they examine the short-term outcomes and learn from them. These outcomes should drive their curiosity about how to further improve the results. This, in turn, helps them to ask the right questions of research or experts who can help. The adult learning is therefore a by-product of measuring effectiveness in the short-term: "Did that work? For whom did it not work? Why not? Where can we find out how to help specific student groups more effectively?" Instead, we commonly see a generic approach to adult learning—such as everyone attending a course that has some general relationship to the goal. That is not the kind of learning that is embedded in a cycle. In a cycle, the short-term outcomes, also known as *quick wins, small wins, just-in-time data*, or *intermediate outcomes*, largely drive the adult learning, as they reveal what teachers and leaders know and do, and what needs to change.

Inquiry Overload

Finally, the last and most common misunderstanding, from our point of view, is that many schools overload teachers with expectations to carry out individual "inquiries" or cycles, as well as school-wide or department-wide ones. If the system is well designed and under-pinned by whole-school or department goals, that approach can be fruitful. But all too often, time is wasted as teachers' inquiries are frequently focused on teachers' interests, with little linkage to the overall improvement goal the school is pursuing. Sometimes teachers must produce a formal report or present their results to the school, but without these inquiries being linked to a shared goal, the sharing of the learning will have little effect on the practice of other teachers or systematic improvement of practices across the school. Too often, individual inquiries become little more than acts of compliance by busy teachers.

Implementing improvement cycles is a team sport; it requires that teams of teachers define common problems and common goals for student learning, design measures, and implement an agreed and consistent strategy to address problems and improve outcomes. Then they need to *collectively* assess their impact in a short period of time, study the trends in their results, and problem-solve before setting off on another cycle. If this work is not collaborative, the learning is not applied and embedded in new school systems. They remain a strat-egy for one teacher, and other teachers do not have ownership of the learning.

All these problems contribute to schools often trying hard but seeing little impact. This book addresses these and other interpreta-tion issues by drawing on optimal aspects of the widely used *Plan-Do-Study-Act (PDSA)* cycle and the *Spiral of Inquiry, Learning, and Action*. Both offer different strengths. The PDSA offers a very clear guide to the sequence of some essential early steps in the process, while the spiral encourages us to be open-minded and to inquire into the causes of problems quite purposefully. It also explicitly highlights the need for teacher learning as part of the process. We endeavour to bring the strengths of both cycles together to create a clearer guide to action for educational leaders who wish to make quicker progress in their improvement efforts.

What Are We Proposing?

Our School Improvement Cycle entails four major steps, just as many other improvement cycles do (see Figure 0.3). Ours starts with *define the problem and the goal.* For the second step, however, we acknowledge how messy (but important) this next analysis and planning step is in improvement cycles, as it entails a number of key steps, all of which are required to develop a theory for improvement. We thus call this step *develop the theory for improvement* and highlight four sub-steps, which we argue are critical for success, but are often forgotten or poorly executed.

- narrow the focus to quick wins;
- develop and test measures of success with the quick wins;
- establish the baseline on quick wins to understand the status quo;
- analyse the causes and design improvement strategies to address the causes.

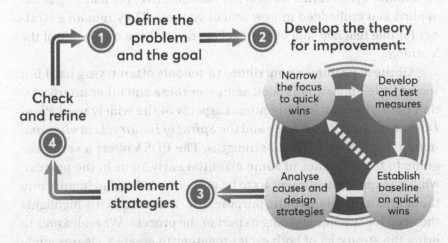

Figure 0.3. The School Improvement Cycle

We accentuate the need to narrow the goal focus to short-term outcomes or quick wins and the need to develop and test specific measures of quick wins, because these provide assurance that the school is moving in the right direction during the year. In addition, a thorough causal analysis is required to address the short- and long-term systemic causes of the problem. These steps of designing and testing measures and carrying out causal analysis feed back into leaders' thinking about what strategies are required to achieve progress. Research is often required to inform an effective pedagogical response. A school may go around this mini-cycle a number of times. For example, the school might first test the theory about what to improve (the initial quick win) and the measurement tool with a few students. If the data collected on quick wins do not show the needed improvement, the school circles back to the first sub-step. This might lead them to revise their thinking about what the focus of initial quick wins should be, and therefore, the measurement tool would have to be adjusted—along with some of their theorising about the causes of the problem. At some stage during this process, the school team needs to stop and formally record their theories about the causes of the unsatisfactory results that they are seeking to address. This leads to the formalisation of a "theory for improvement" that entails both pedagogical and organisational strategies that are theorised to lead to improvement.

In the third step, *implement strategies*, the team implement their agreed strategies, potentially first in one or two classrooms to test them further, collecting quick win outcome data and process data about changes being made by teachers and leaders as they do so. They then move to the fourth step, *check and refine*, looking at the results they achieved and what they have learnt from the implementation that could support the refinement of their measures and strategies in the next cycle.

The School Improvement Cycle is repeatedly followed, with new learning occurring in each cycle, and ultimately leads to a solution that becomes embedded into business-as-usual (Langley et al., 2009). Based on our recent research into schools implementing the School Improvement Cycle (Bendikson et al., 2020; Le Fevre et al.,

2020; Meyer et al., 2020), and our practical work supporting cohorts of schools over many years, we have developed this cycle to clarify how this process seems to work best in practice, placing a particular emphasis on the early steps that either set the school up for success, or lead to frustration and lack of concrete results if they are missed.

How Is the Book Set Out?

The book is organised as follows:

Chapter 1—Introducing the School Improvement Cycle
The chapter provides an overview of our School Improvement Cycle and its steps. It exemplifies an improvement cycle with an example from the health context.

Chapter 2—A Case Study of Gauguin Primary
The chapter provides a case study from a primary school demonstrating a "target student" approach using the School Improvement Cycle.

Chapter 3—A Case Study of O'Keeffe College
A case study from a secondary school is described. It demonstrates a "common needs" approach using the School Improvement Cycle.

Chapter 4—Defining the Problem and the Goal
The chapter describes the problem analysis involved in deciding on an initial goal focus for improvement.

Chapter 5—Developing the Theory for Improvement
An overview is provided on how a theory for improvement is developed iteratively.

Chapter 6—Narrowing the Focus to Quick Wins
The reader is guided to refine their goal to a narrow "wedge" of the larger annual goal, the quick wins. These are also referred to as *small wins, intermediate outcomes*, or *just-in-time data*.

Chapter 7—Developing the Measures and Establishing the Baseline
School leaders are guided into the types of practical measures of quick wins that schools typically utilise. A range of practical examples used by schools is provided.

Chapter 8—Analysing Causes and Designing Strategies
This chapter describes the process of carrying out a causal analysis and designing aligned strategies to address the causes.

Chapter 9—Implementing Strategies
Typical strategies that school leaders use are described, including professional development, the development of benchmarks, standardisation of practices, and the development of documentation. The need for the development of systems is emphasised.

Chapter 10—Checking and Refining
Schools' methods of checking their results and refining their actions are described.

Chapter 11—Leading Improvement: The Human Side of Change
This chapter describes the conditions and associated leadership necessary for successful school improvement, including how leaders can sustain change over time, build a culture of improvement in their school, and deal with resistance to change.

It's not rocket science, but it can be incredibly difficult to help leaders carry out this School Improvement Cycle process. This book aims to make it easier. Like many concepts that seem plain in writing, it can be more difficult to execute in practice, given the usual challenges that are involved in successfully leading a diverse group of people in complex environments. We have seen few, if any, leaders who have not been challenged in their efforts to gain a visible impact on learning outcomes. Overcoming the challenges takes not only a set of specific actions, but also the development of a set of attitudes. These include: courage to focus narrowly on important outcomes; determination to put in place rigorous monitoring processes; and perseverance to stick with the long game and not lose focus. In the last chapter of the book, we thus provide guidance on the human side of leading improvement and dealing with challenges that may arise.

References

Bendikson, L., Meyer, F., & Le Fevre, D. (2020). Goal monitoring: A crucial lever to achieve school improvement. *SET, 2*.

Bryk, A. S., Gomez, L. M., Grunow, A., & LeMahieu, P. G. (2015). *Learning to improve: How America's schools can get better at getting better*. Harvard Education Press.

Bryk, A. S., Sebring, P. B., Allensworth, E., Luppescu, S., & Easton, J. Q. (2010). *Organizing schools for improvement: Lessons from Chicago*. The University of Chicago Press.

Cardno, C., & Piggot-Irvine, E. (1996). Incorporating action research in school senior management training. *International Journal of Educational Management, 10*(5), 19–24.

Gawande, A. (2011). *The Checklist Manifesto: How to get things right*. Profile Books.

King, M. N., & Kovacs, J. (2015). *Improving learning*. Quality Learning Australasia.

Langley, G. J., Moen, R. D., Nolan, K. M., Nolan, T. W., Clifford, N. L., & Provost, L. P. (2009). *The improvement guide: A practical approach to enhancing organizational performance* (2nd ed.). Jossey-Bass.

Le Fevre, D., Meyer, F., & Bendikson, L. (2020). Navigating the leadership tensions in creating collective responsibility. *Journal of Professional Capital & Community, 6*(3), 253–266.

Meyer, F., Bendikson, L., & Le Fevre, D. (2020). Leading school improvement through goal-setting: Evidence from New Zealand schools. *Educational Management Administration and Leadership, 1*(19), 1–19.

Mintrop, R., & Zumpe, E. (2019). Solving real-life problems of practice and education leaders' school improvement mind-set. *American Journal of Education, 125*, 295–344.

Moen, R., & Norman, C. (2010). Evolution of the PDCA Cycle. *Basic Quality*, November.

Piggot-Irvine, E. (2009). Action research as an approach to development. In E. Piggot-Irvine (Ed.), *Action research in practice*. NZCER Press.

Tichnor-Wagner, A., Wachen, J., Cannata, M., & Cohen-Vogel, L. (2017). Continuous improvement in the public school context: Understanding how educators respond to plan-do-study-act cycles. *Journal of Educational Change, 18*, 465–494.

Timperley, H., Kaser, L., & Halbert, J. (2014). *A framework for transforming learning in schools: Innovation and the spiral of inquiry*. Centre for Strategic Education.

CHAPTER ONE

Introducing the School Improvement Cycle

In the following chapter, we introduce the School Improvement Cycle that this book is based on and provide an overview of the different steps in the cycle. We illustrate the cycle with an example from the health sector by surgeon, writer, and public health researcher Atul Gawande, who is well known for his book *The Checklist Manifesto*. Working through an example from a different context can help in understanding the main ideas and their application without getting entangled in the detail and the thinking about one's own context. In the following two chapters, we provide case studies of a primary school and a secondary school we have worked with to show the application of the School Improvement Cycle in the education sector.

What Is the School Improvement Cycle?

An improvement cycle is a systematic approach to achieving continual improvement. As noted in the Introduction, our School Improvement Cycle entails four major steps: (1) define the problem and the goal; (2) develop the theory for improvement; (3) implement strategies; and (4) check and refine (see Figure 1.1). While our School Improvement Cycle entails four major steps, as most other cycles do, it adds detail to the important early step of developing a theory for improvement. We unpack this step into four sub-steps, including how to narrow the focus to *quick wins*, which are also known as *lead indicators*. These are short-term outcomes aligned to the larger goal that is being pursued. It is in these sub-steps where most of the planning occurs when implementing improvement cycles, and this is where the foundation is laid for success or failure. Next, we provide a short description of each step and sub-step in the cycle and illustrate them with examples.

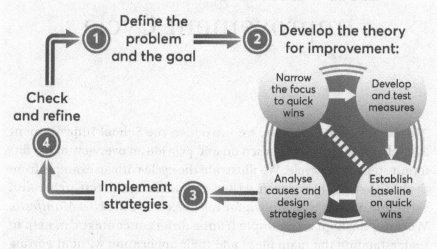

Figure 1.1. The School Improvement Cycle

Step One: Define the Problem and the Goal

For this first step, leaders are asked to pause and think about what the problem is that they are trying to solve, and what improvement they want to see. This often entails reviewing the school's strengths and weaknesses in academic and other valued student outcomes by scanning the school's current and past results and any qualitative data, such as samples of student work, classroom observations, or views of students, their families, and teachers that the school may have collected through surveys or other means. But this very wide type of scan can lead to paralysis in decision making due to the huge amount of data. Schools get stuck as to what all the data mean and where they should start.

We recommend that schools start by focusing on academic student outcomes. In this step, leaders identify the key area where improvement is needed. Leaders in most schools will already have a hunch about this. They check this hunch by scanning the academic data, looking at them from different angles (e.g., subject, gender, ethnicity, year level), and comparing it with data from similar schools or national benchmarks. This will prompt a further look into the wider qualitative data—but this can be deferred until the problem is clearly defined.

Once the priority problem or gap in outcomes is identified, leaders can define the goal. The goal is simply the inverse of the problem. For example, if the problem is a low level of numeracy achievement, the goal would be to *"Improve numeracy achievement"*. The main goal can remain general, but it can include the specific group of students such as *"Improve numeracy achievement, especially for Māori"*. The goal can also focus on other types of academic outcomes such as *"Reduce drop-out rates"* if the main problem identified was high levels of student drop-out. Once the main goal is identified, specific targets can be set by putting a number on where the school wants to be at a certain time point, for example, *"Increase written language achievement by 20% by the end of the year"*. A specific target is motivating teachers and students to have something to work towards.

Step Two: Develop the Theory for Improvement

A theory for improvement sets out the detailed plan on how to achieve improvement in the identified problem area in both the short- and long-term, and how this improvement will be measured. The key task in this step is carrying out causal analysis. We recommend schools use the *fishbone diagram* invented in post-war Japan; it is still a powerful tool. However, we have found that it is a good idea to start by testing out a few theories about the possible nature of the initial quick wins before moving on to a formal causal analysis. By carrying out this process, school personnel develop their thinking about some of the various causes of the problem.

Developing a theory for improvement entails four sub-steps: (1) narrow the focus to quick wins; (2) develop and test measures of the quick wins; (3) establish a baseline on the quick wins; and (4) analyse causes and design strategies to address causes of the problem. These strategies include any organisational or structural changes needed to support the pedagogical improvements, such as documenting agreed standards or changing expectations of a leadership role. To develop a theory for improvement that is eventually relevant to the whole school, schools might have to go around these sub-steps more than once to refine and check their theorising about causes, as well as the adequacy of their measures and strategies.

Narrow the Focus to Quick Wins

Narrowing the focus to quick wins entails narrowing down the goal to smaller, identifiable gains on the problem. To narrow the focus, further analyses might be needed on what the problem is, or what is contributing to the problem. There are two approaches to narrowing down an improvement goal to quick wins. A school can focus on what we call a *common needs approach*, which entails identifying a skill that is a common concern across many students. Alternatively, a school can use a *target student approach* focussing on improving outcomes for a specific student group, either using completely individualised quick wins, or, more commonly, still focusing on common needs across this group.

For example, with a common needs approach, if the goal is to improve numeracy achievement, there might be specific skills that most students are lacking (e.g., counting, problem-solving, using fractions), and quick wins can focus on these areas. If a high drop-out rate seems to be partly due to students not having confidence about their ability, a focus on developing that confidence might be a first quick win. In contrast, if the school finds that specific groups are underachieving, or wants to focus on students generally underachieving in a learning area, a target student approach might be used. It requires identification of a small group of students with higher needs who are the focus of intense teaching and monitoring to assess the effect of the current teaching strategy. If changed pedagogical practices are impactful with target students, there is confidence that they can be successfully applied with all students.

Develop and Test Measures

The quick win must be measurable in some easy way to check prog-ress. Quick-win measures should be good predictors of the lon-ger-term outcome measures of the goal that the school is seeking. These long-term results are also known as *lag indicators*. These are usually the end-of-year results reflected in secondary school qualifi-cations or in relation to agreed national standards or standardised achievement test results. For that reason, *lead indicators*, or mea-sures of quick wins, are required during the year to provide assur-ance that the school is on track for success. Measurement tools can be rubrics, checklists, small assessments or tests, or surveys, and should be easy and quick to implement and analyse. In the case of numer-acy achievement, schools might use rubrics or checklists to "tick off" quick-win skills students have mastered, or tasks completed. In the case of the drop-out example, the school might collect data on stu-dent confidence in the first week of term with a short survey with a 1–5 rating scale on their confidence of achieving a passing grade in the course, complete certain assessments, or understand specific mate-rial provided. Ideas for measuring quick wins are best tested initially on a small group of students to see if the quick-win idea really is prob-lematic and whether the proposed measurement tool works. While there could be critiques of over-assessment, these measures are good examples of assessment for learning; they allow teachers to monitor progress, and they inform next teaching steps, rather than acting as a summative assessment of learning.

Establish the Baseline on Quick Wins

Establishing a baseline requires identifying the current or initial level of achievement using the quick-win measures. This step is usually part of testing the measures, but it is also important to document where students are starting out so that it is clear as to what prog-ress they are making. Collecting this baseline data is also part of test-ing hunches about the problem. For example, a school could collect data on students' ability to count, if teachers and leaders have a hunch that students are missing this skill and it is impeding their progress in numeracy. But, upon testing their measurement tool (e.g., a checklist of different aspects of counting), the school might find that this is indeed a problem, or it might not be, or only one aspect of it might be problematic, such as counting backwards. If that were the case, they would amend their measurement tool to collect just that information and test again. Now, knowing they were on the right track for an initial quick win, teachers can consider reasons for their lack of prior knowledge of this, and for the unsatisfactory results from the lag indicators.

Analyse the Causes and Design the Strategies

The next step is to formally investigate and document the systemic causes of the problem and think about how these could be addressed. The causes of the problem can be identified through a *root cause analysis*. This means inquiring into why students are lacking these skills, or why they are lacking confidence and dropping out. Causes often lie in the organisation and management of the learning environment—such as a lack of clear guidance for teachers, no standardisation of best practice, no documentation of agreed practices, inadequate or uneven teacher knowledge, and a lack of systems to closely monitor student progress. All of these are the responsibility of school leaders. To identify the causes and check that they are valid, schools need to examine the data in more depth. It is at this step where leaders often look into the qualitative data they have, or collect data to understand the problem. Involvement of students and teachers in the causal analysis is critical, because every stakeholder will have a different perspective to add to the understanding of the nature of the problem.

Once the potential causes are identified, schools decide on improvement strategies that will address these causes. The alignment of strategies to problem causes is important, since schools often implement an array of strategies that will not solve the problem because they do not address the major causes. Furthermore, schools usually need to take a multi-pronged approach to addressing multiple root causes, meaning they need to implement a few strategies (e.g., pedagogical, organisational) at the same time or in sequence.

These need to focus on a common goal—the improvement goal the school has set—otherwise energy and focus get divided and schools fall into two different types of traps. One is what Bryk and colleagues (2015) referred to as *solutionitis*: the tendency to try multiple solution strategies and test the efficacy of none of them. The second is a phenomenon described by Mintrop and Zumpe (2019), who found that, despite their efforts to encourage principals to use a rigorous approach to causal analysis, the principals' biases associated with past practices overshadowed their ability to analyse causes and align solutions. Instead, they fell back on solutions from their past.

It is useful to first test the effectiveness of an improvement strategy on a small group of students before scaling up and implementing the strategy team-wide. For example, in the case of numeracy, teachers could trial a different approach to teaching problem-solving for a few weeks and measure progress. If deemed successful, the approach can be taken to other classrooms, or, if unsuccessful, the approach might need tweaking, or more data might be needed on what could be done differently to address the problem before implementing the approach more widely. In developing strategies, leaders and teachers should turn to research and internal and external expertise to establish what the best possible solutions are.

Improvement strategies that involve systemic changes in the organisation or school management can often not be trialled; instead, they need to be implemented school-wide to achieve coherence. This more formal development of the longer-term theory for improvement is converted into a simple one- or two-page improvement plan. It guides the leaders' longer-term actions, whereas the quick-win data drive the short-term pedagogical changes.

Step Three: Implement Strategies

This step refers to the implementation of the improvement strategies' team- or school-wide. It usually entails teachers carrying out one or two agreed pedagogical practices and reporting back at regular meetings. At the same time, leaders need to address the systemic issues in their theory for improvement—for example, issues in the organisational structure such as changes to meeting schedules, roles, and responsibilities.

It is important to develop new routines as part of the *implementing strategies* step. This is not a project. Schools develop routines to embed a way of working and need to timetable key milestones to be met. For example, schools set dates for the teacher meetings to examine quick-win data (e.g., every 3 or 4 weeks) and for professional learning meetings to address common pedagogical needs of teachers. During this step, data on quick wins for the students (*outcome data*), as well as data on the effectiveness of the implementation of the agreed strategies (*process data*), are collected.

Step Four: Check and Refine

In the final step of the cycle, the data are reviewed, trends are summarised, and implications discussed to inform the implementation of the next cycle and to update the improvement plan. Schools typically use cycles of 3, 5, or 10 weeks at the longest, before data on the quick-win results and the effectiveness of the implementation are reviewed. Secondary schools often find the 10-week term a useful length of time for a cycle, as each department has limited time with students. Primary schools tend to use 3–5-week cycles, so there are at least two per term. If the cycles are more than 5 or 6 weeks in length, it is advisable to have some reporting about half-way through the cycle.

In the case of trying to increase numeracy achievement, and more specifically students' skills in problem-solving in a primary school, teachers might report on the strategies they are using and how they see them impacting their students' learning after 2 or 3 weeks. This provides some *process data*; it lets leaders know that teachers have tried the agreed strategies. It also provides some initial data from teachers about what they are learning. After 5 weeks, the cycle is formally completed, and teachers share their experiences and results of the quick wins. The teachers might decide on some practices that were particularly effective. All teachers might then focus on the use of these strategies in their next cycle. The data and the discussions about effective processes and strategies become the basis for refining their teaching approach.

As actions become routine, new structures are embedded and progress is made towards the improvement goal. Given that schools are usually looking to improve significant long-term results, iterative cycles tend to refine practices until results are at the desired goal level before turning to a new goal. We have known schools to focus on one goal for 18 months or more. At other times, 3–6 months have been adequate before schools moved on to another goal.

Cycles, by their very nature, are intended to be moved through quite rapidly. The first time a cycle is used will take longer, because staff need to learn to use key tools in the process (e.g., the fishbone, cause-strategy charts or driver diagrams, graphs of results, measurement tools). It also takes time to put key organisational conditions and documentation and monitoring structures in place to facilitate the improvement work in the early cycles. Once these conditions are created in the early cycles, later cycles become much quicker and more focused on implementing strategies and reviewing quick-win results.

Depending on which cycle and what time of the year, data from end-of-year assessments (or any other long-term measure that was decided on as a lag indicator) can be used to check long-term progress. The ultimate test of the validity of the theory for improvement will be in the lag indicators—did the quick wins along the way result in the improvement that was sought?

Implementing the School Improvement Cycle

For improvement cycles to be effective, they must be efficient and non-intrusive in that they just become part of the way schools do things. They are not an extra. That cultural shift comes from implementing the cycles multiple times. Once the routines, structures, and habits that underpin cycles of improvement become established, schools' improvement becomes continuous.

Given the multitude of pressures on principals and other school leaders, if the cycle is not embedded, the improvement goal is likely to be forgotten over the course of the year or the improvements lost once a new goal is set (Bendikson et al., 2020). Using improvement cycles provides leaders with a structure for carrying out both major and minor improvement initiatives.

The implementation process runs alongside "business-as-usual". Teachers may teach what they have always taught, but they would add one new strategy to their repertoire. It would require them to use one quick-win measure at the beginning and end of a short cycle. For example, teachers trying to improve reading comprehension may have a theory that improving the ability to locate information within text would improve inference skills and, therefore, overall comprehension skills. Their quick win, therefore, would be to improve the students' ability to locate information. They would design a measure of that ability, such as a short text with multi-choice or open-ended questions, to gather baseline data. They would teach those skills directly and have a post-assessment at the end of the cycle. This implementation work runs alongside or as part of their normal teaching.

Next, we illustrate the use of an improvement cycle in a health context. There are many lessons to be learnt from the health sector's use of data to drive cycles of improvement.

The School Improvement Cycle Illustrated in a Health Context

Public health processes frequently do not match the gold standard required to preserve life. This is not due to lack of care or lack of knowledge, but hospitals are complex and busy organisations requiring a lot of different people to work together at different times and to carry out multiple procedures on a number of different patients. A priority problem in the health context is not a lack of knowledge about what should be done for patients, but rather the inability to routinely ensure that certain procedures occur at the right time and in the right way to the right people. The complexity of pursuing this goal is described in Atul Gawande's 2011 book *The Checklist Manifesto: How to Get Things Right*, and in the excerpt below:

> Here, then, is the fundamental puzzle of modern medical care: you have a desperately sick patient and in order to have a chance of saving him you have to get the knowledge right and then you have to make sure that the 178 daily tasks that follow are done correctly—despite some monitor's alarm going off for God knows what reason,

despite the patient in the next bed crashing, despite a nurse poking his head around the curtain to ask whether someone could help "get this lady's chest open". There is complexity upon complexity... so what do you do? (pp. 28–29)

This complexity seems comparable to the complexity in classrooms and schools. In education, we too must deal with multiple complexities and often know what is needed to help students improve, but the sheer number of conflicting challenges divert leaders and teachers from systematic improvement efforts. The School Improvement Cycle helps leaders and teachers to enact improvement in a purposeful way amidst the day-to-day pressures.

What follows is our description of Gawande's tale put in the context of our School Improvement Cycle. Through this description, we illustrate key features of the cycle, and how improvement is focused on systems and processes rather than people. Most people know what to do, but without systems there is too much variability in their approaches to get optimal outcomes.

Define the Problem and the Goal

The first step of any improvement cycle is articulating the priority, client-centred problem and defining the goal. In Gawande's situation, the priority problem was defined by the World Health Organisation, which had identified that surgeries were increasing world-wide, but so was the number of associated unnecessary deaths. For example, Gawande reported that, in the United States, half of the 150,000 deaths following surgery were preventable. Thus, the problem was "*Too many preventable deaths*", and the goal was the inverse of that: "*To reduce preventable deaths*". This is a lofty goal.

Develop the Theory for Improvement

Gawande's identification of the problem and a goal, as well as his team's measurement and strategy development, align with what we see as the development of a theory for improvement and its four steps. The first step in developing a theory for improvement is to identify what is causing the problem, and how quick wins can be identified and measured. For data, Gawande had the number of avoidable deaths following surgery, but little more. Thus, a first step for Gawande's team was to interview people who were implementing these processes and systems. Gawande's team heard varying theories about problems occurring in operating theatres and what contributes to preventable deaths around the world. It seemed that surgeons knew what to do in surgical procedures, but the right procedures were too often carried out incompletely or inconsistently. Gawande reported that "The knowledge exists, but however supremely specialized and trained we may have become, steps are still missed. Mistakes are still made" (p. 31).

Narrow the Focus to Quick Wins

Thus, the quick win that Gawande thought to address was the inconsistency in basic processes in surgeries. As he stated: ". . . we rarely investigate our failures. Not in medicine, not in teaching, not in the legal profession. . . . A single type of error can affect thousands, but because it usually touches only one person at a time, we tend not to search as hard for explanations" (pp. 132–133). He and his team identified six typical errors to address in surgical procedures: the timely delivery of antibiotics, the use of a working pulse oximeter, the completion of a formal risk assessment for placing an airway tube, the verbal confirmation of the patient's identity and procedure, the appropriate placement of intravenous lines for patients who develop severe bleeding and, finally, a complete accounting of sponges at the end of the procedure. The quick wins were the fidelity with which each of these steps was taken.

Develop and Test Measures and Establish a Baseline on Quick Wins

Gawande's team employed and trained local researchers to monitor the number of deaths in surgeries in eight very different hospitals around the world. Of close to 4,000 patients undergoing surgery, 400 had major complications, and 56 died. These were baseline outcome data on the overall goal. They also gathered process data to find out where each surgical team's "failure points" were. This entailed documenting on a simple yes/no checklist where surgical teams either failed to take the six safety steps before, during, or after surgery, or where they failed to carry them out in a timely way. This documentation was their *baseline data* for each quick win. Given that they were simply looking at the completion of behaviours, developing a measure was simple. Yet Gawande noted: "These are the basics, the surgical equivalent of unlocking the elevator controls before airplane take-off. Nevertheless, we found gaps everywhere" (p. 145).

Analyse Causes and Design Strategies

For Gawande, one cause of the problem lay in the complexity of the work in surgical theatres, and thus a solution was needed to reduce complexity by clarifying and focussing surgical teams on basic procedures. Looking at other industries where the work is complex and risky and where certain tasks need to be carried out in the right order at the right time, such as in flying planes and building skyscrapers, he noted that checklists were frequently utilised. Thus, there was ample evidence that checklists were successful in improving outcomes in multiple complex and high-risk situations.

Data from previous research into surgical checklists and surgical teamwork, along with many small trials in their own surgeries, led Gawande to theorise that a "spoken"—rather than a written—checklist was required. As they trialled these ideas themselves, they found other small issues to resolve. For example, who would take charge of ensuring the checklist was used? Who would read it out? They followed the example of pilots where the pilot who is not flying the plane takes over the driving of the checklists. This approach disperses leadership across the team. The team trialled having a nurse read out the checklist, which proved effective and empowered nurses to show leadership and to question surgeons if steps were missed.

In his causal analysis, Gawande also reflected on research about the nature of teamwork in operating theatres. Surgical teams in large hospitals are often comprised of individuals who have never met before. Yet they are all required to contribute to a successful surgery. In reality, though, the surgeon is the most powerful player on the team, and nurses may hesitate to question a surgeon, given the power differential. However, earlier research into the levels of communication within surgical teams showed that in cases where staff knew each other's names, communication during surgery and job satisfaction were rated higher. Furthermore, when nurses were given the opportunity to mention concerns at the start of surgery, this lessened the occurrence of problems.

Thus, a fuller theory of improvement started to develop, including a focus on how to improve team dynamics in operating theatres. The idea of ensuring formal introductions of everyone at the start of any surgery and providing everyone with the opportunity to comment on the patient's history or the procedure before starting were key strategies.

Implement Strategies

Having formally trialled their processes and established their baseline level of performance, the checklist process was implemented in eight pilot hospitals: four in developing and four in wealthy countries. Gawande's team introduced and trained surgical teams in each hospital to use the checklists. The core parts of their strategy were a professional learning strategy to teach teams to use the checklist effectively, and a monitoring strategy. The hospital leaders made presentations to surgical staff and provided them with their previously collected baseline data on their processes, showing that their current procedures lacked consistency. Their theory for improvement essentially hypothesised that, if people learnt where problems occurred in their own surgeries, they could, and would, remedy them. They encouraged the pilot hospitals to introduce the new Safe Surgery Checklist into one operating theatre initially, and one where the chief surgeon operated to work out any problems in their context before branching out to other theatres and to ensure that senior surgeons would drive the general uptake of the checklist.

Check and Refine

Gawande's team travelled the world to observe in the operating theatres and to gather feedback from surgical teams. The stories they heard gave them hope that the checklist would be successful. There were reports of better teamwork, and the final results of the trial indicated a 36% drop in complications, and deaths fell by 47%. Even in the wealthier countries, complications from surgery in the pilot hospitals dropped by 33%. An anonymous survey of 250 staff after three months showed that 80% found the checklist to be easy to use and something that improved care, while 93% agreed that they would want the checklist used if they were undergoing surgery. Some of the hospitals had to make some minor changes to the checklist for it to work in their context. Some found that they needed to address some systemic issues in their context to be able to implement the use of the checklist, such as an undersupply of equipment. The next year, the Safe Surgery Checklist was scaled up.

Conclusions from the Public Health Sector

There are multiple lessons to be learned from this example of Gawande's and from other public health tales such as the management of pandemics. One is that improvement efforts need to focus on how the work is done in order to improve an outcome. It is not just about improving the practice of surgeons but improving how the work is organised and supported. The same is true in education. Problems do not all lie in the quality of teaching, but rather in how that teaching is organised, monitored, and supported by leaders.

Another lesson is that of complexity. Like the health sector, education has more knowledge and tools than we can practically come to grips with. It is complex work. None of us has the capacity to learn and know all that is available to help us carry out our role. Changes in staff, context-specific challenges, and just trying to keep up with compliance activities such as maintaining health and safety can easily divert the focus of leaders away from a systematic method of improving, even if they do know that one exists.

So, does this process work in education? And more importantly, does it work in schools where there are no researchers to guide the work and collect the data? The answer is "Yes". In the next chapters, we illustrate how two schools have managed this process with very little external help.

Key Points

- Improvement cycles entail the major steps of defining a problem and a goal, developing a theory for improvement, and implementing strategies, and checking and refining them in light of the quick-win data.
- Cycles are iterative. They often start with small "tests" of a change idea and a measure, perhaps by one teacher, before scaling up to be used by a group of teachers.
- Improvement cycles are enacted alongside "business-as-usual", but ultimately become "business-as-usual" because new routines and practices are systemised.

References

Bendikson, L., Broadwith, M., Zhu, T., & Meyer, F. (2020). Goal pursuit practices in secondary schools: Hitting the target? *Journal of Educational Administration, 58*(6), 713–728.

Bryk, A. S., Gomez, L. M., Grunow, A., & LeMahieu, P. G. (2015). *Learning to improve: How America's schools can get better at getting better*. Harvard Education Press.

Gawande, A. (2011). *The checklist manifesto: How to get things right*. Profile Books.

Mintrop, R., & Zumpe, E. (2019). Solving real-life problems of practice and education leaders' school improvement mind-set. *American Journal of Education, 125*, 295–344.

CHAPTER TWO

A Case Study
of Gauguin Primary

This chapter describes one primary school's efforts to improve by implementing improvement cycles over several years. We provide a brief description of the school and then describe each step taken.

Context of Gauguin Primary School

"Gauguin Primary School" is an urban school with approximately 450 students in Years 1–6 (5–11 years old), 50% male and 50% female. The students' ethnicity is approximately 55% New Zealand European, 35% Māori (indigenous New Zealanders), and 10% other ethnicities (e.g., Asian; students of Pacific Island descent).

Like other New Zealand schools, Gauguin Primary has a high degree of autonomy. The national curriculum is a broad, guiding document with eight learning areas. While all primary schools must deliver on these learning areas, they are free to design and assess the curriculum as they choose. Many primary schools use what is called "Overall Teacher Judgments", commonly referred to as OTJs, to make summative assessments in reading, written language, and mathematics. Teachers make these judgments using multiple sources of assessment data to decide whether students are "below", "at", or "above" a standard for their age group. The standard is defined by the individual school based on high-level indicators in the national curriculum. Level 1 is approximately equal to the performance of students in the first two years of school, Level 2 is the performance level in the third and fourth years of school, and so on.

Define the Problem and the Goal

The first step in the improvement cycle is to examine the available school data to define the priority problem and set an improvement goal. An analysis of OTJs in Gauguin Primary showed that, while mathematics outcomes had improved over the previous years, outcomes in reading and written language were low, with only half of the students achieving at the expected level in written language. Further, in written language, boys and Māori students were underperforming relative to girls and students of other ethnicities. Underachievement in written language was, therefore, the obvious priority problem to focus on, given the relatively low outcomes and the inequities in outcomes. Thus, the school's initial, overarching goal was *"To improve written language"*.

Develop the Theory for Improvement

Developing a theory for improvement entails four sub-steps: narrow the focus to quick wins, develop and test measures, establish the baseline on quick wins, and analyse the causes and design the strategies for improvement aligned to the identified problem causes.

Narrow the Focus to Quick Wins

There are two approaches to narrowing an improvement goal down to quick wins. A school can focus on a *common needs approach*, where staff focus on a skill that is a common area of concern across all students, or the school can use a *target student approach* focusing on improving outcomes for a specific group of students. In the latter case, quick wins are usually individualised. The senior leadership team (SLT) at Gauguin Primary chose the target student approach and narrowed down their goal to about six target students per class. They asked all teachers to identify as a target student any learner who was approximately a year behind expected achievement levels. The team did not discount the needs of students who were performing at even lower levels, because the school already had teaching interventions in place for these students. The expectation was that the target students had the potential to reach the required level in a relatively short timeframe with more specific and intensive teaching.

While all classes had about six target students initially, if new students enrolled in the school who were performing a year or two below expectations, teachers would add them to their target group. Students stayed in the target group until they were at expected levels of achievement, but teachers continued to monitor them regularly to ensure they did not slip in their achievement. Using a target student approach means that teachers can focus, monitor, and test changes in practice for a small group of students rather than the whole classroom before embedding changes into their wider practice.

The quick wins were small improvements in target students' written language work. The long-term measures or lag indicators were OTJs in written language as a summative end-of-year assessment. Here, the school looked at improvement across the school not just at the target students, as the improvement made with these students should affect overall outcomes.

Develop and Test Measures

Gauguin Primary asked teachers to set individual quick-win targets for each student; these had to focus on a specific skill in written language that the student was lacking. The SLT was very conscious of the fact that it was asking teachers to adopt a new practice and wanted to involve teachers deeply in the creation of the system. Thus, the decisions about the specific targets for each student were initially left entirely to teachers. However, after testing this approach, the SLT agreed that it did not provide enough certainty on progress, as there was too little coherence or consistency in the targets. The wide range of targets made it challenging to get a clear idea of progress. Therefore, whilst undergoing their early cycles, the SLT concurrently created a document that articulated clear progressions in some aspects of written language to enable teachers to measure progress in a coherent manner. These progressions were drawn from national literacy progressions but were refined down to core outcomes that were perceived to be limiting factors if not addressed in a timely way. The school's written language progressions were organised into four categories: (a) message making; (b) structure of language; (c) spelling; and (d) legibility of writing. In the next iteration of testing their approach to quick wins, the students were to focus on at least one deep feature and one surface-level feature of writing from the school's new guidelines. When reporting on students at the end of each 5-week cycle, teachers had to report each student's goals as "achieved", "partially achieved", or "not achieved".

Establish the Baseline on Quick Wins

The baseline was established by recording how many target students were operating at each level of the progressions. Progress was measured by the degree of movement by students through the written language progressions. The principal collated a summary of what was being focused on and how many students were achieving their individual targets across the school. He mapped where target students sat at different levels of the progressions and whether they had moved. The collated data were reported back to staff at quarterly school meetings, where implications and next steps were discussed.

Table 2.1 depicts how clear and measurable individualised targets were defined for each student in a 5-week cycle. Teachers used this form to mark students' progress. They then attached it to a student's "real work" (e.g., a photocopy of something they had recently written) as evidence that the student had sustained mastery of the skill(s). This evidence was handed to the principal, who kept the samples on file to review against future samples.

Analyse Causes and Design Strategies

When it comes to the causal analysis, most leaders start with some initial theories about what is causing a problem and how to address these causes; however, leaders need to be open to differing ideas at this step to ensure that all possible causes are considered. The SLT at

Table 2.1. Example of Progression Rubric for a Target Student

Progressions worked on		Level	Achieved	Partially Achieved	Not Achieved
Message Making	Write a message with several clear ideas (write 3 sentences that relate to each other)	Lliii	√		
Structure	Regulate punctuation, where most sentences will start with a capital letter and end with a full stop (Write 3+ sentences with a capital letter and full stop)	Lliii	√		
Next step progressions to work on					
Message Making	Write a message with several clear ideas (write 6 sentences that relate to each other)	Lliii			
Structure	Include a mix of simple and compound sentences	Lliii			

Gauguin Primary had an initial theory that the quality and consistency of pedagogy was one root cause of the problem that had to be addressed. In their causal analysis, this initial theory was backed up by observations of classroom practices by the external audit agency, the Education Review Office (ERO), which also reported inconsistent practice in teaching written language.

To look further into causes of the low achievement in written language, the SLT examined a range of data, including their own in-class observations, teachers' comments on student reports to parents, student work samples with teacher feedback, and student voice data. They also reflected on school processes for measuring progress. These data sources are shown in Table 2.2 alongside the causes identified in the data and the strategic responses linked to each cause. A table such as this can be a useful tool for keeping an overview of the analysis and ensuring that strategies put in place are addressing the identified causes. As can be seen in the table, the SLT identified several causes that were pedagogical (e.g., lack of knowledge on how to support students, and topics used), but also organisational (e.g., lack of shared understanding of achievement levels across the school, and lack of a short-term monitoring system).

A multi-pronged approach is typical of improvement work, as problems tend to have multiple causes that need to be addressed at different levels of the school system. For example, while Gauguin Primary had a strong initial theory about a lack of teachers' pedagogical knowledge to address specific student needs, they also acknowledged that, to date, they had not put in place the conditions to ensure greater teacher focus and consistency of practice. In relation to the pedagogical causes, the SLT decided on professional learning and coaching as strategies that would both motivate and empower teachers and build their pedagogical knowledge. In relation to the organisational causes, the SLT made changes in structures, such as creating "pods" or small groups of teachers for coaching, implementing systems for monitoring quick wins, and creating progressions of core written language skills to promote consistency in expectations and understanding of achievement at each level. Some of these strategies were designed up-front (for example, the organisation of teachers' pods), while others were developed as the staff learnt from each cycle (for example, the need for explicit school progressions against which to measure progress).

Implement Strategies

Next, we expand on Table 2.2 to describe the key strategies taken by the school to achieve improvement in more detail and show how they link to the causes of the problem.

Inconsistent Teaching Practices: Create Organisational Conditions to Enable Coaching and Close Monitoring of Target Students

The long-term success of the new approach would not have occurred without two major innovations in school organisation. The first was

Table 2.2. Causal Analysis: Data, Identified Causes, and Strategic Responses

Data	Identified causes	Strategic responses
In-class observations by SLT and External Review Office (ERO)	Inconsistent teaching practices.	**Changes in organisation:** Create organisational conditions to bring teachers together in pods for coaching. **Professional learning:** see below
Teachers' comments on student reports to parents	Some teachers did not know how to help students improve. Students were experiencing the same problems year-on-year.	**Professional learning:** Deepen teacher knowledge through coaching on how to get sustainable improvement in written language.
In-class observations	Teachers lacked sense of agency.	Provide professional learning on effective pedagogy.
Teacher feedback on student work	Teachers lacked understanding of what was an appropriate level of achievement at each year level. Teacher feedback to students was sometimes not providing next steps and was not always followed up on.	**Changes in expectations:** Create progressions of core Written Language (WL) skills to promote consistency in what is valued, taught, and measured. Next learning steps for each target learner clarified and recorded for student and teacher use.
In-class observations by SLT and ERO	Teaching was targeted predominantly at whole-class or group level.	**Individualised approach:** Individual needs addressed and monitored through target student approach. Improve detail in planning of WL lessons.
Reflection on school processes for measuring progress	Teachers could not measure their effectiveness in teaching WL in the short-term.	**Measurement:** Measure and report on target students against progressions.
Student voice	Students were not motivated by the topics.	**More student choice of topic:** Students use writing to communicate about topics of interest.

the creation of teacher *pods*. Teachers were organised into seven pods of two or three teachers, as opposed to the three larger, year-level teams (junior, middle, senior) in which the teachers had historically met. These teacher pods allowed for in-depth coaching (by senior leaders) of teachers who worked at the same level of the school, because the school was able to release two or three teachers, but not five to eight teachers at the same time.

The second innovation was the school's decision to fund one release day per term for every teacher, in addition to the two fully funded days provided by the government. This commitment allowed up to three teachers in each pod to be released for 1 day every 3 weeks. Only a third of that time was required for the quick-win monitoring and planning of next steps. As one deputy principal noted: "We took one of three periods of the day to talk about written language. The rest of the time was for the teachers for planning and marking". This made the change attractive for teachers. Obviously, not every school would be able to fund such teacher-release. However, finding the resources to do so is a testimony to the priority that the SLT placed on being able to bring teachers together. It is a case of strategic resourcing. The school prioritised enabling teacher collaboration over, for example, paying external facilitators to support the professional development of the teachers. They could do this because the SLT had the knowledge and capability to coach the teachers, but the time and structure required to ensure its success was the problem to solve.

The decision to increase teacher release time had a positive impact on both the ability to work systematically with teachers, but also to enhance teacher buy-in. It demonstrated that teachers were valued. In return, teachers were expected to engage with the in-depth coaching and monitoring. The principal was able to argue: "We are going to invest in an extra day's release per term if you work with us in an intense way on this improvement focus".

Lack of Pedagogical Knowledge in Written Language: Provide Professional Learning

The school used a two-pronged approach to professional learning: coaching focused on written language teaching in pods and whole staff professional learning focused on more generic pedagogical skills but informed by the results and practice gaps in written language. These whole staff professional learning sessions, while specifically aimed at enhancing written language results, had the benefit of improving teaching across the curriculum areas, not just in written language.

Teachers had pod meetings every 3 weeks in which they worked with their coach, who was one of the deputy principals. They used student work to reflect on the question *"How effective was my teaching?"* and spent a lot of time examining inputs and outputs: what teachers did and what students achieved. As one deputy principal said two years into this approach: "Teachers can't escape . . . but they love it. It has become just the way they do things". Initially, the coaching sessions were largely directed by the deputy principals who had in-depth knowledge in written language. Later, teachers took more control in driving the process.

In the pod meetings, the deputy principals would sometimes spend half an hour helping teachers on a shared focus and the rest of the time meeting teachers individually. The meetings had tight agendas, as the following example in Table 2.3 shows, but the organisation of that time varied according to teachers' needs.

Table 2.3. Example of Agenda Items for a Pod Meeting

Agenda/Foci	Discussion	Follow-up actions and timeframe
Data take 1	Look at data from pod year levels in core area to see trends.	Use graphs to predict and promote achievement. Present analysis at the next meeting.
Graphs update	Shifts over time? Any concerns to discuss?	Track these students in daily planning. Moderate with Pod before assessing as "achieved" at the next meeting.
Term 2 writing samples	Reflect on principal's analysis of the data. Discuss any specific points.	What points will you pick up for your programme? Discuss what you tried at the next meeting.

In addition to student data, the two deputy principals used formal observations of teachers as data to feed into their coaching sessions at both pod and whole-school levels. Sometimes the observational focus was driven by the teacher—for example, "I'm working with this group and I would like some feedback on . . ."—and sometimes the focus was driven by the deputy principal—for example, "I'd like to see you working with [student], helping him to increase his writing volume in a writing session". Thus, the feedback given to teachers following observations was deeply connected to outcomes discussed in coaching sessions. The formal observations were carried out twice per term, were formally timetabled, and were clear on the agreed focus of the observations. The overall trends from observations, or recommendations based on the trends seen in pods, were summarised by the deputy principals and were the focus of whole-school professional learning meetings. The excerpt in Table 2.4 demonstrates how these were summarised as trends.

While the intensive coaching was focused on how to accelerate the progress of target students, much of the professional learning at

Table 2.4. Summary of Trends from Observations

Focus	Summary
Planning	• Need to be clear about teacher actions (overt instruction) and writing opportunities for students to practise intended learning (multiple exposures). Step out what you will do, what the students will do. Know who you will work with and when. • Expectation that all planning is on Google docs—you should refer to your plan as you teach.
Feedback	• Need to shift from using feedback as a reminder for writing to verification to the student that they are applying the skill their goal is focused on. • If there is no change in student application of a skill, rethink instructions or identify prerequisite skill.
Support systems	• Some rooms are literacy-rich, with lots of language-based work displayed and referred to in learning. • All rooms have spelling supports, but not all students habitually use them as part of their essential toolkit.

the school was initially focused on research findings on effective pedagogy that impact teaching in any curriculum area. The SLT used whole-school meetings and "teacher-only days" to introduce eight quality teaching strategies compiled in a succinct review of Hattie and Marzano's research (Killian, 2021). The eight "powerful strategies" include: a clear focus for the lesson; overt instruction; having students engaging with content; giving effective feedback; multiple exposures of concepts; having students apply their knowledge; students working together; and building students' self-efficacy. The staff analysed what their written language sessions would look like if these principles were effectively applied. Thus, Gauguin Primary sought to gain an understanding at a broad level of how to improve teaching effectiveness but applied the research directly to the written language context. Again, the SLT took responsibility for leading the professional learning.

Unclear Expectations: Develop School Progressions

Developing a common set of learning progressions at each curriculum level was a fundamental step in driving the improvement, given that a lack of knowing "next steps" and inconsistent teaching practices had been identified as causes of the problem. The progressions offered a simple, but clear, outline of major learning outcomes, allowing student progress to be more precisely targeted and measured. The school's version comprised six levels, four of which were focused on the first curriculum level, which encompasses achievement in Years 1 and 2 at school (Levels pre-L1, L1i, L1ii, and L1iii), and two focused on Level 2 and Level 3 of the curriculum, for students in Years 3 to 6. An example of one level of the progressions is illustrated in Table 2.5.

Teaching at the Whole-Class Level: Implement Target Student Approach and Improve Planning

At the beginning of the process of implementing cycles, the SLT at Gauguin Primary felt that teaching was too general and not targeted enough to individual student needs; thus they adopted the target

Table 2.5. Example of One Progression Level: Level 1i

Aspect	Skill
Legibility	Correctly form some letters.
	Become aware of different letter sizes (tall, half, tails).
Message making	Tell a simple clear message to write (oral or written).
Structure	Write left to right.
	Begin to space words.
Spelling	Use known symbols to record a message.

student approach and use of the progressions. Beyond that, the SLT dictated little about how teachers should teach. The one thing the SLT mandated, beyond the close monitoring of target students, was the nature of teachers' planning. Such planning had to (a) be specific; (b) respond to their teaching context with appropriate strategies; and (c) have a clear focus for each lesson. As the senior leaders explained: "They [the teachers] were always good at planning for reading and mathematics but not for writing". Teacher planning for individual students was expected to be detailed and referred to in lessons, and was reviewed in coaching sessions.

Inability to Measure Effectiveness: Measure Against Progressions

All teachers had to provide graphs of their target students' progress to the deputy principal before each pod meeting, so the deputy principal could check whether the students had progressed or not. Teachers would put the data up on a screen during pod meetings and talk about the implications of the data for each of their target students. The pod's data were open to everyone. The ability of teachers to now see clearly where students sat on the progressions against the school's expectations helped teachers to assess their own effectiveness.

Students not Motivated by Topics: More Student Choice

The principal held the view that much of the writing tasks students were given by teachers was of limited interest to students and did not reflect his desire to see writing as authentic authorship of ideas. Students' feedback validated this theory. Some students were asked to write on such topics as "What I did on the weekend". The principal felt that writing was about expressing views and ideas and needed to be a genuine opportunity to capture thinking that would be shared with an audience. Those expectations were made clear to teachers and, as a result, students were given more authentic opportunities to write, and time was invested in students re-crafting writing and then sharing it with others.

Check and Refine

To check and refine practice after each cycle, the principal initially collected work samples from each target student every 5 weeks. He tallied up the type of goals and the degree to which they were achieved—that is, the number of students who achieved their goals, the different levels of the goals, and the breakdown by gender and ethnicity. He summarised the trends for each school level and compared the data to those of the previous cycle. The data were reflected upon (relative to what worked and where gaps persisted) to identify next steps and potential changes in practice.

By the third year, the principal asked the teachers to do their own monitoring of target students twice per term, using student samples. As the cycles were sustained, teacher growth was occurring and, with it, teachers developed efficacy and a desire to take more control. In turn, the SLT felt that teachers had the capability and knowledge to take more of a leadership role in responding to the quick-win data. Over the 3 years, this was one of numerous procedures that were refined in Gauguin Primary. For example, in the first year the principal was involved in the pod meetings, but by the second year, he moved to a role of analysing the samples and discussing the trends with the whole staff, leaving the coaching of pods to the deputy principals. Deputy principals, in turn, found themselves doing less talking, as teachers were increasingly driving the process: "The teachers will spontaneously get the graphs out and do the talking in pod meetings". The progressions were also developed and refined over time.

The case of Gauguin Primary highlights that a theory for improvement is not developed up-front and in one go, but is refined over time. Learning from each improvement cycle drives further innovations or refinements to the improvement process and strategies.

Quantitative Results

Improvement is not always obvious. In the first year that Gauguin Primary worked on written language, their OTJs, which they used as lag indicators, improved in all subjects, but were better in reading and mathematics than in written language. The SLT attributed this to three things. First, the focus on improving pedagogical strategies was applicable in all subjects. The eight core strategies, referred to earlier, had impacted results in all subjects. Second, the SLT theorised that OTJs in reading improved because the students had to read and re-read their writing in order to craft it. Thus, the focus on writing also incorporated a stronger focus on reading. Third, they believed that teachers' baseline OTJs in written language were not very reliable or consistent, as teachers had lacked a shared understanding of what achievement in written language looked like at the beginning of this process. Through the work with progressions, teachers developed their ability to judge the written language levels, and OTJs became more rigorous and consistent across the school. Thus, earlier OTJs in written language may have been more generous than those in the later years in their improvement journey. This demonstrates the importance of building a shared understanding of assessment measures.

Overall, the OTJ lag data showed improvement in written language over three years. Students achieving at or above expected level went from 64% to 76% (see Figure 2.1). Gender differences were also reduced (see Figure 2.2), but results for Māori students, though improved by 11%, still revealed a stubborn equity issue requiring res-olution (see Figure 2.3).

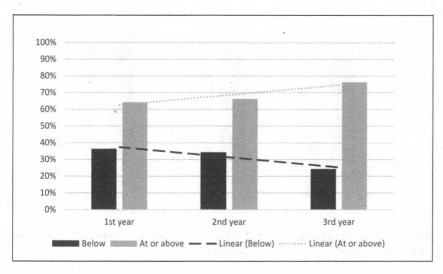

Figure 2.1. Written Language OTJ Achievement in Percentages Comparing "Below" with "At or Above"

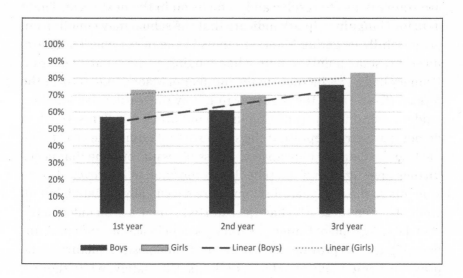

Figure 2.2. Written Language OTJ "At or Above" Achievement in Percentages by Gender

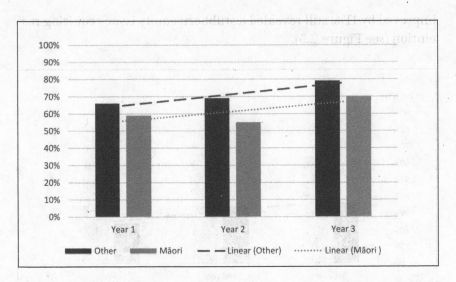

Figure 2.3. Written Language OTJ "At or Above" Achievement in Percentages by Ethnicity (Māori Versus other Ethnicities)

Graphs such as these illustrate the importance of leaders cutting the lag data by gender and ethnicities to investigate whether there are equity issues to resolve and to focus on in the next cycle. These data for Gauguin Primary indicate that the school may benefit from purposefully targeting Māori students in the next cycle. There are, however, some points to note when looking at these data. Gauguin Primary had a 15% increase in the number of Māori students over the 3 years (from 112 in the first year to 132 by the third year). Further, students continually transition in and out of schools. Thus, the data do not necessarily represent the same students from one year to the next, so the data are indicative of a possible issue, but one that needs further investigation if the school is to continue to improve. Also, no students in the first year of school were specifically targeted, but all students, even those who have just started school, are included in the OTJ data. A graph of Gauguin Primary's data in actual student numbers (Figure 2.4) provides a more accurate and positive picture of the progress being made for Māori students. Ultimately, while there is still room to improve the equity of results, the quantitative data are validating the SLT's theory for improvement.

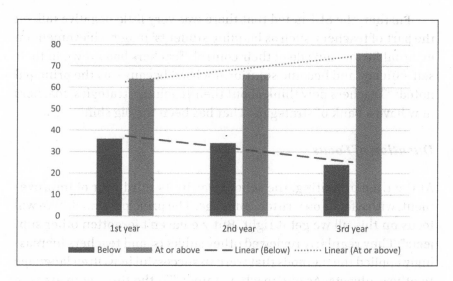

Figure 2.4. Number of Māori Students Achieving 'Below' or 'At and Above' in Written Language

Qualitative Results

The positive shift was seen not only in the quantitative results, but also in the attitudes of teachers and students, as indicated by the qualitative data collected, such as writing samples, teacher feedback, and student voice. By the third year, all students were producing a far greater volume of written language. All students seemed to love writing and saw themselves as writers. Writing was shared and celebrated regularly, for example, by being read out at assemblies or published in the school newsletter for other students to read. Every student had their writing published in some way.

Teachers were more confident and knew what progress should look like. The target student approach and progressions provided clarity for teachers. They also found their teaching tasks to be more manageable, because student achievement goals had been narrowed down, and focusing on teaching towards these goals seemed more achievable. As one teacher noted, "You are not trying to cover everything. You are homing in on particular things".

Further, the SLT noted that there was very little negative talk on the part of teachers, such as blaming students' underachievement on external factors outside of their control. Teachers had grown in their self-efficacy and become solution-focused because, as the principal noted: "Teachers now think about their teaching strategies; teachers now have a bank of strategies. That has been the big shift".

Duration of Focus

At the time of writing, the school was in its third year of improvement, with a focus on written language. The principal stated: "We will focus on this till we get it right. But we haven't forgotten other subjects". They regularly reviewed other subjects, and teachers increasingly applied the methods that were so successful in written language to other subjects. As one teacher stated: "So the three core areas of reading, writing, and mathematics, every pod meeting we are discussing those and looking and discussing what is working and what is not. And we have had a huge shift".

The School Improvement Cycle approach has become the tool that Gauguin Primary employs to ensure continuous improvement. What the school is confident about is that: (1) they have improved pedagogically; (2) the organisational practices have been refined to support that success; and (3) the staff is committed to continuing the hard work of focused improvement efforts. That is not to say that everyone who has worked in the school has liked and adapted to this approach. Some staff who were new to the school found this way of working difficult; they were supported, but they could not handle the rigour and moved on. Those who stayed, or came to the school and learnt this way of working, became advocates for the approach, and 3 years later, much of the ongoing improvement was being driven by teachers themselves.

References

Killian, S. (2021). *8 Strategies Robert Marzano & John Hattie Agree On*. Evidence-Based Teaching. https://www.evidencebasedteaching.org.au/robert-marzano-vs-john-hattie/

CHAPTER THREE

A Case Study
of O'Keeffe College

In Chapter Two, we exemplified a *target student* approach to quick wins in a primary school setting. In this chapter, we illustrate a *common needs* approach that is operated at the department level of a secondary school. We provide a brief description of O'Keeffe College and then describe each step taken in the School Improvement Cycle, with an emphasis on the milestones they used as quick wins.

Context of O'Keeffe College

O'Keeffe College is a city school in a low-income community with approximately 1,200 students in Years 9 to 13 (13 to 17 years old). Approximately one third of the students are of Pacific Island descent, 12% are Māori (indigenous New Zealanders), and the remainder are mostly New Zealanders of European descent.

The Senior Leadership Team (SLT) comprises the principal, three deputy principals, and three assistant principals. The SLT is supported by a large group of middle leaders, some of whom are *curriculum leaders*, such as heads of faculty and heads of department, while others are *pastoral leaders* who manage student discipline and wellbeing.

In New Zealand schools, students must pass the National Certificate of Educational Achievement (NCEA) to access tertiary education or apprenticeships. NCEA is a standards-based qualification system that is internally and externally assessed. It involves three qualification levels. Level 1 is assessed in Year 11 (students' third year at secondary school), Level 2 is assessed in Year 12 and is the level necessary

49

to enter polytechnics or further training, while Level 3 is necessary to enter university. New Zealand also has a separate University Entrance (UE) qualification, which entails meeting certain compulsory Level 3 standards, including numeracy and literacy. Schools typically try to support all students to attain at least Level 2. A previous government had a target of 85% of all students achieving Level 2 qualifications, and many schools adopted this target.

O'Keeffe College has enjoyed a steady enrolment increase over recent years because of new housing developments in the area, and probably its growing reputation for academic rigour. The school has been using improvement cycles for 5 years and, as a result, its outcomes are now significantly higher than those of similar schools. As part of those improvement cycles, they have implemented numerous strategies: they improved their goal clarity by having just one clear academic goal each year; they reorganised the roles of SLT members so that all senior leaders are responsible for overseeing and improving academic outcomes; and they established close monitoring systems to track results during the year and initiate problem-solving mechanisms for common causes of failure. The SLT has altered the school's courses and pathways for students to improve their chances of success. The school has seen improved literacy and numeracy outcomes for all students, improved attendance, and reduced lateness.

The following case study illustrates their actions in implementing the School Improvement Cycle in what we are referring to as Year 4 of this work, so that we can show their results in perspective over a 5-year period.

Define the Problem and the Goal

The first step in the cycle is to examine the available school data to define the priority problem and set an improvement goal. O'Keeffe's data showed that their positive results were not equitable across ethnic groups. They wanted to ensure that every student could experience success. The problem they saw was that *not every student was successful in each of their courses*. Thus, the school's initial goal in

Year 4 of their improvement journey was *"every student will achieve in each course"*, which is essentially a 100% target.

There are potential benefits and challenges with such a visionary goal. For a goal to inspire staff commitment and to be motivational, it needs to be challenging yet attainable (Locke & Latham, 2013). Arguably, 100% is not attainable. The benefit is that teachers are asked to work hard to help every student succeed, whereas if there was a target of 90%, for example, a teacher could think about who are the 10% unable to succeed, and not put effort into these students' success. If staff, however, see the bigger picture in the aspirational goal, 100% could be motivational and a culture-setter that says: "We value all learners".

Develop the Theory for Improvement

While O'Keeffe College experienced success in the previous 3 years, it was still challenged to motivate some students to attend school and to make the necessary effort to succeed. While a school can improve many systems to optimise student success, students themselves still must do the work to be successful. A key question for the school has been "How can we increase students' motivation?"

Narrow the Focus to Quick Wins

The SLT thought that an alteration to their approach to quick wins might help. The school had already instituted a system of closely monitoring internal assessments for Level 1 to 3 qualifications as their quick wins, but they wanted an approach that would also motivate students who were in pre-qualification classes, and students who did not always pass formal assessments. They sought an approach that would help motivate every student regardless of year level and/ or previous success. The SLT decided to place emphasis on students' completion of key minimum *milestones* in each course. The milestones were key outcomes particular to any given course. For each course, teachers had to identify up to three measurable milestones a student needed to achieve to be successful in their course within a 10-week term. Examples that the SLT used when this idea was initially presented to staff were: handing in two essays; completing three artworks; delivering an oral presentation; demonstrating a skill. Staff needed to be clear on what outcomes they viewed as critical to students' longer-term success in their courses: "How do students count their quick wins and how does an individual teacher say, 'Right, these kids are on track'?" (Deputy Principal). This is an example of a common needs approach, as it identifies needs or key learning outcomes across students in each course. Little (2002) noted that departments are often undervalued as a force for reform, but they are the appropriate vehicle for improvement in secondary schools, given their departmentalised nature.

Develop and Test Measures

Outcomes were tracked in the central student management system with just a Yes/No beside the student's name. This record of the student's achievement of the milestones was printed and sent to parents at the end of each term. It highlighted whether the student had done the necessary work to be on track for future success in a course (see Table 3.1 for an example). A student's progress report had five or six subjects with between one and three milestones, or quick wins, per course. The lag indicators were the numbers of students passing a course at the end of the year.

O'Keeffe College asked teachers to set these milestones and test them in the first term of the year. The types of milestones teachers designed varied from those that simply required students to complete a task, such as "Complete a reading log for the term," to those that required a task to be both completed and to attain a certain standard.

At the end of the first term, the approach was reviewed and refined. Curriculum leaders from each department were asked to comment on positives and negatives for students, teachers, and leaders. Teachers reported seeing improvements in some students already. It was making the learning process much more visible to students. Students knew that if they completed those tasks, they were more

Table 3.1. Example of How Milestones Were Recorded in the Student Management System

Student	Art Complete 1 sketch	Art Complete 1 painting	Science Write 800 words explaining the physics principles behind motion with three key points.
John	Yes	No	Yes

likely to succeed. They found the milestone report at the end of the term motivating. They were thrilled to get a printout with a "Yes" and dismayed when they got a "No" and wanted to be able to do what was required to change the "No" to a "Yes". Parents also benefited from a very concrete, easy-to-understand, and timely indication of whether their child was doing what was required at school to be successful. On the negative side, some students struggled to understand what was required, because some teachers and curriculum leaders themselves struggled to be clear about milestones. Teachers learnt a lot from this first test of the process. They were able to quickly identify "at-risk" students and to put in a process for re-teaching and re-submitting a task. When sharing data, all teachers could see quickly how a student was performing in other courses. Thus, when other departments were getting better results with a student, they could learn from that.

The biggest lesson from this first test of the approach was that teachers needed to be clear about the *must do* or *must know* requirements of the milestones. Teachers needed a better understanding of what the big markers of progress in their courses were and then align the milestones to these markers. As one of the SLT stated, milestones could be "a quantity of something produced, it could be at a certain quality, but what it has to be is something that tells these students they are on track to achieve in this course".

This initial test showed that curriculum leaders needed to be careful about the nature of milestones. They needed to be predictors of success and not be too large. One or two milestones per course seemed optimal. Further, it highlighted some teachers' needs in relation to pedagogy and classroom practices and allowed curriculum leaders to support teachers in a timely fashion. The curriculum leaders could use the milestone data in their meetings with teachers and problem-solve early in the year to help students succeed. On the downside, curriculum leaders initially felt overloaded, as they were stressed about teaching their own classes and meeting other administrative requirements whilst implementing this new system.

Furthermore, the school found that the milestones that focused only on task completion—as opposed to achieving a certain standard—were optimal for enhancing teacher and student motivation. If a student completed a task but not to the required standard, and therefore saw a "No" next to their name, they were not always motivated to put in further effort. The teachers who reported success in this early cycle found that students who typically handed in nothing now wanted to hand in something to receive that "Yes". Just completing the task was a major accomplishment for some students, and often the initial "Yes" led them to put more effort in to gain more success in the next milestone.

Curriculum leaders also decided to change the nature of the milestones during the term and not wait for the next term if they realised their first effort was not appropriate. They also wanted a full description of the milestone in the student management system for visibility. They agreed that they would map out all the milestones for their courses ahead of time in the following year. This imperfect first effort taught them how to maximize the benefits of the milestone approach.

Establish the Baseline on Quick Wins

Given that the school had used a simple Yes/No measure, it was incredibly easy to see how many (and which) students achieved all milestones and which students were tracking well for end-of-year success. As one member of the SLT said: "We always think 'they will catch up later', but they don't"; thus the monitoring of early progress was recognised as important in ensuring later success.

Analyse Causes and Design Strategies

The SLT launched the causal analysis with a full day's workshop with all teachers at the beginning of the year. They started by sharing the school's latest data disaggregated by gender and ethnicity. While they had good results overall, results for Māori students were concerning. They asked departments to identify students who had not achieved in their courses and to discuss potential reasons for their underachievement.

In groups, teachers were asked to think of their individual practice and to analyse what they, as an individual teacher, could do to ensure that every student experienced success. Next, department groups were asked to consider what they could do as a department to improve outcomes for every student by thinking about the causes they had identified. Each department came up with a few strategies.

The Arts, Careers, Dance, Drama, and Music course teachers banded together for this exercise, as they were small departments. They experienced some interesting challenges. They argued, for example, that some students ended up in their courses not because they wanted to be there, but because of timetable challenges. Therefore, some of their students were not motivated to succeed. This theory was reinforced with data showing issues with attendance and meeting deadlines. Initially, their response was to "filter" who could enter their courses. However, the conversation ultimately turned to how they could redesign their courses for "alternative needs" to make them more attractive to students. Course redesign and better student placement in courses were identified as strategies across the departments.

In another case, the mathematics department highlighted mainly organisational causes impeding the achievement of all students, as Table 3.2 illustrates.

The SLT also reflected on their leadership effectiveness. They identified some common causes of current under-achievement that could be addressed, as can be seen in Table 3.3. One cause related to middle leaders' professional leadership capability (e.g., not seeing themselves as problem solvers; not confident in running focused and efficient data-based meetings with their teams). Another cause

Table 3.2. Causal Analysis: Data, Identified Causes, and Strategic Responses
for the Mathematics Department

Data	Identified causes	Strategic responses
Teacher observations	Poor basic mathematics vocabulary	**Changes in pedagogy:** Create list of basic words and their meanings to be learnt by all students.
Teacher observations	Some students struggle from the beginning of the course because they do not have enough prior exposure to concepts. By the time this is recognised, it can be too late to change course.	**Changes in organisation:** Start courses with the same basic content to encourage early success and to check that students are in a course that will enable them to succeed. This allows students to change classes early in the year if necessary.
Teacher discussions across departments	Some students are displaying maths skills in other courses but are not getting recognition for the maths part of their tasks, e.g., graphing in social sciences.	**Changes in organisation:** Co-curricular data collection to be used for maths so that all students' maths achievements are recognised.

related to the need to have quick wins across the school, not just in the
qualification years (Years 11–13). They looked for more precise data
and a measure that could be used across all years (Years 9–13). Hence,
they decided to trial milestones as a quick-win measure. They also
wanted to make their monitoring and support of middle leaders more
robust and to put more emphasis on celebrating student success.

Implement Strategies

Next, we expand on Table 3.3 to outline the key strategies taken by
the SLT in more detail, to achieve improvement and to show the link
to the hypothesised causes.

Lack of Confidence and Skills in Leading a Team: Leadership Training for Middle Leaders

All curriculum and pastoral leaders attended 9 half-day sessions of
leadership training over the course of a year and a half to help develop

Table 3.3. Causal Analysis: Data, Identified Causes, and Strategic Responses Carried Out by SLT

Data	Identified causes	Strategic responses
Feedback from curriculum leaders; observations by SLT	Some curriculum leaders lack confidence and skill in leading teams and never had leadership training.	**Professional learning:** All curriculum leaders undergo leadership training, including basics such as running a meeting and problem-solving.
Reflection on strength of Year 9 and 10 outcome monitoring	Quick wins currently only measured in qualification years, not across the whole school.	**Changes in organisation:** Use milestones in every course across the school to make student learning visible.
Reflection by SLT on the rigour of their past practice	Insufficient accountability and support for heads of faculty.	**Changes in expectations of heads of faculty and organisation:** Create more oversight: Meetings with heads of faculty at beginning of every term to review milestone data; SLT to meet with one head of faculty individually every Friday to provide an opportunity for more general discussion and support.
Review of current processes with staff	No timely or adequate celebration of student success with students and families.	**Changes in organisation:** Send milestone report to parents each term. Have certificates for students who meet all their milestones in a term. Use assemblies to celebrate success.

their leadership skills and their sense of efficacy. They learnt some basic leadership theory and had the opportunity to discuss their leadership issues in a safe environment. The returns on this investment were evident when middle leaders discussed what they needed to do to create a better system, and collectively approached the SLT not with their problems, but with their recommendations for improvement into how they operated as a critical group of leaders. Because they participated in the professional development together and developed a shared theory of leadership, they were more empowered and motivated to initiate further improvements, such as organising their own meetings so they could share effective practices.

Need to Have Quick Wins across the School: Use Milestone Approach at All Year Levels

As discussed earlier, O'Keeffe had previously used internal NCEA assessments for quick wins and had tracked those results closely, but there was no method of tracking progress in the junior years, or during the year in externally assessed NCEA courses. Many students entered the school with below-age-appropriate levels in literacy and numeracy, yet there was no agreed way of closely tracking outcomes in these critical early years. The milestone approach could be applied to any year level and to all courses.

Insufficient Accountability Systems and Support for Heads of Faculty: Meetings Between SLT and Heads of Faculty

The SLT felt that they could increase accountability for results across the school and provide more support for faculty leaders in problem-solving. They instituted two new meetings largely based on the new milestone data. At the beginning of every term over the course of 3 days, they had a 1-hour meeting with every head of faculty. Heads of faculty could bring along any head of department or teacher to help reflect on results from the milestone data from the last 10-week term. An SLT member described a potential discussion: "You've got 30 kids, and 60% have not met the first milestone. What are we going to do about that, because that is an indication that the students are not on track to successfully complete this course?" Some heads of faculty found this "no place to hide" approach somewhat challenging at first, but eventually most saw the benefit of having the SLT's ear and support to solve teaching-related problems in a timely manner.

Throughout the term, the SLT would also meet with one head of faculty for an hour every Friday. This meeting was more general and provided the head of faculty the opportunity to talk to the SLT about any matter of concern to them. One deputy principal commented that this meeting really helped to build relational trust. This was because there was no hard-and-fast agenda beyond what the middle leader wanted to raise. They had the whole SLT there to hear any concerns and help solve problems of any type that affected them, whether it be about equipment that was needed or issues with staff or students.

Inadequate Timely Celebration of Student Successes: Create Celebrations

Milestones were a perfect instrument for motivating students. They allowed students to experience early and visible success. The SLT wanted to see certain levels of achievement in those milestones being publicly recognised. They developed certificates and had students walk across the stage to receive them. This was well received by both students and parents: "It is like a sticker chart, when you talk to parents they say, 'Yeah, we've got all the certificates'" (Deputy Principal).

Check and Refine

In the *check and refine* stage, the school reflected on the organisational changes they had made and reviewed the quantitative and qualitative results. The milestone approach was refined as previously described in the *develop and test measures* section.

Organisational Structures

After the completion of the first cycle, where the nature of a good milestone had become clearer to staff and had been refined, other improvements were deemed necessary. For example, the school had to raise the bar for what to celebrate and where to celebrate student success. As more and more students attained all milestones each term, their successes were celebrated in their regular house assemblies, as opposed to the whole-school gatherings.

Middle leaders changed the nature, timing, and purpose of their meetings. For example, the pastoral leaders wanted to become more coherent in their approach to improving attendance and behaviour and needed to meet separately from the heads of faculty and heads of department. Finding time for meetings is challenging in large and complex schools but, to become more unified in their approach, the middle leaders needed longer and more regular meeting times to discuss the progress of the student cohorts that they were overseeing and to ensure that they were consistent in their expectations of students.

Faculty and department heads needed to work with their teams of teachers to review milestones from each term and to address ongoing concerns with either individual students or individual teachers. They applied their training on running effective meetings and problem-solving to improve the coherence and performance of their departments or faculties.

Quantitative Results

Improvement is not always dramatic. When improvement systems are developed over time, growth in lag-indicators occurs incrementally as the ongoing cycles continue to turn more and more potential into actual outcomes. Assessing improvement over time with different student cohorts can occur in numerous ways. In the case of O'Keeffe College, the school's final results at Level 2 and for University Entrance were key to enabling students' access to further education. Thus, our analysis focuses on those qualifications to illustrate the school's improvement in performance over time.

At O'Keeffe College, the data show some quick shifts in improvement and then incremental improvements over the next 5 years. Research from the United Kingdom, using value-added methods that account for differences in socio-economic conditions, indicates that secondary school performance usually does not alter greatly in many schools over time and, when there is improvement, it is usually incremental and typically develops over 3 or, at most, 5 years before performance once again dips (e.g., Gray and Thomas, 2001; Thomas et al., 2007). Then a *ceiling effect* becomes evident, meaning that improvement levels off, as is little room left for improvement. Thus, if a school is already high-performing compared to similar schools, it is very difficult to continue to improve year-on-year. In that case, maintaining high levels of achievement is the appropriate goal. If a school is under-performing, however, and there is room for improvement, some sudden positive shifts in performance can be obtained with initial improvement efforts.

Figure 3.1 shows the school's results at Level 2 and University Entrance for 5 years. In Year 2 of their improvement journey, the school had a jump in the University Entrance results it was focusing on that year, and it has since continued to improve those results incrementally. Year 4 of their improvement journey represents the first year of implementing the milestone approach. Here they showed moderate improvement in University Entrance, but they did not see an immediate impact on Level 2 results. By Year 5, both Level 2 and University Entrance results continued the overall trend of improvement.

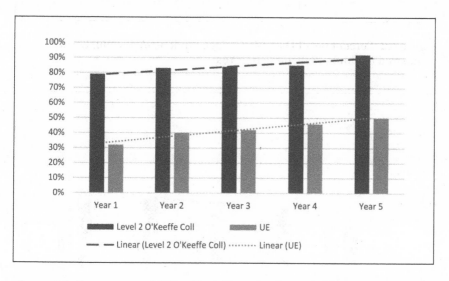

Figure 3.1. Percentage of O'Keeffe College Students Achieving Level 2 and University Entrance (UE) over 5 Years

One way of assessing a school's effectiveness is to compare it to schools with similar socioeconomic settings (Bendikson et al., 2011). This is the approach we are using. Figures 3.2 and 3.3 show O'Keeffe College's results compared to similar schools. By the fifth year, O'Keeffe's students were out-performing students in similar schools by 12 percentage points in Level 2.

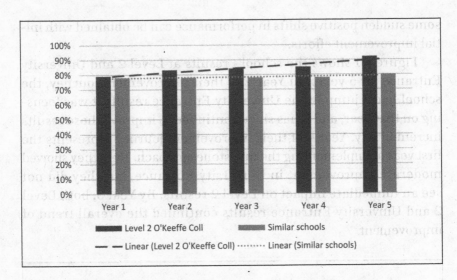

Figure 3.2. Percentage of O'Keeffe College Students Achieving Level 2 Compared to Similar Schools over 5 Years

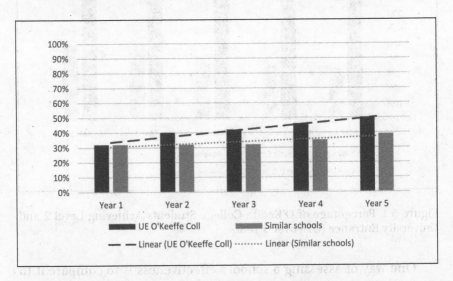

Figure 3.3. Percentage of Students Achieving UE in O'Keeffe College Compared to Similar Schools over 5 Years

O'Keeffe College's University Entrance results improved by 11 percentage points over the 5-year period, while similar schools improved by 7 percentage points. The pattern in these results aligns to the

pattern reported by researchers about long-term trends in secondary schools; it is difficult to sustain an improvement trajectory, and,
where schools are successful, effects are incremental, as schools continue to tweak for systemic improvements. Nevertheless, the trend is
one of increasing differential between O'Keeffe College and similar
schools. Few secondary schools show continual improvement over 5
years—a feat that O'Keeffe has achieved.

While the overall trends are positive and the school is moving
towards its lofty goal of ensuring that *"every student will achieve in
each course"*, it is still a work in progress. Figure 3.4 shows that results
for European and Pacific students have improved between 15 and 20
percentage points, but for the Māori students, there was only a 6%
increase. This highlights that the three ethnic groups started off performing reasonably equitably in Level 2, but the improvement cycles
have not resulted in equitable results, particularly for the Māori students. Pacific students' Level 2 results have improved at a similar rate
to that of New Zealand European students.

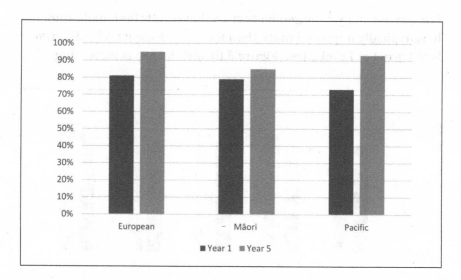

Figure 3.4. Level 2 Results in Percentages by Ethnicity over 5 years

The different ethnic groups' University Entrance results are starker
in their differing trends, as shown in Figure 3.5. Only the results for
New Zealand European students are clearly on an upward trajectory.

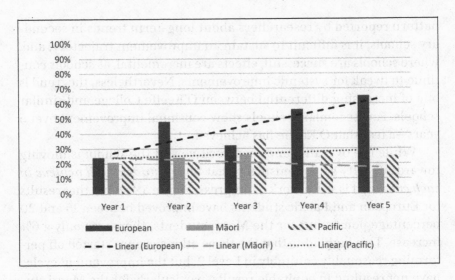

Figure 3.5. University Entrance Results in Percentages by Ethnicity over 5
Years

Further, an analysis by gender reveals that results for female students
have typically improved more than for male students. The difference
is not great at Level 2 (see Figure 3.6), but the gap is increasing.

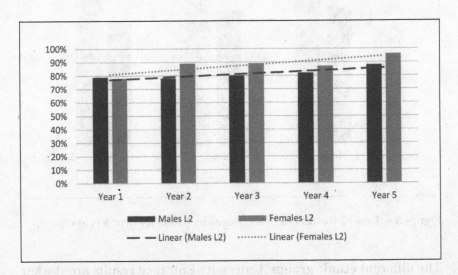

Figure 3.6. Level 2 Results by Gender over 5 Years

The inequity in results by gender is most evident when University Entrance results are examined (see Figure 3.7). Results for male students have improved, but the gap between their results and those of female students has not narrowed.

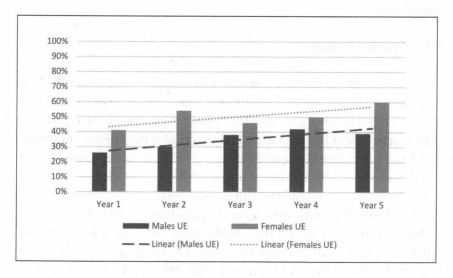

Figure 3.7. UE Results by Gender over 5 Years

These analyses point the way to further areas for improvement for O'Keeffe College. Examining the lag data is the ultimate review and the final step in the improvement cycle where schools can celebrate their successes, but also start to problem-solve on unsatisfactory results. If the data had not been disaggregated, the results would look amazingly good. But, as is often the case, they are not equally good for everyone. Improvement cycles work off these variations in results; they are a source of learning. "Why is there an ethnic and gender difference at University Entrance, and what can be done to improve results of male, Māori, and Pacific students?" This starts the theorising again, and so the next cycle begins. Talking to students, families, and teachers to investigate these patterns is a next step for the college. Explicit investigation of what is impeding these students' progress is now needed, along with research into potential remedial strategies. A *target student* approach may be appropriate for the next stage of their improvement journey. Focusing on what works for specific Māori, Pacific, or male students may be what is required to accelerate the improvement of some students and for the system to learn "What works, for whom, and why?"—the key question in improvement science.

Qualitative Results

A positive shift in results was not only seen in the quantitative lag indicators, but also in the attitudes of teachers and students. Middle leaders reported that the milestone approach was motivating for both the teachers and the students. The external school review organisation, the Education Review Office, reported that student voice helped to shape curriculum courses and pathways, and parents appreciated "teachers' and leaders' timely and responsive communication about their children's wellbeing, engagement, and achievement". The Review Office noted that students at the school achieved valued outcomes that included "a sense of belonging and inclusion in an environment that values diverse cultures, developing wellbeing and self-management" skills, and "confident engagement in learning through positive supportive relationships with staff and peers". Any casual visitor can attest to the positive climate of the school both within classrooms and in the grounds. There is a sense of orderliness, purpose, and family, and a high level of professionalism evident within the staff.

Duration of Focus

The School Improvement Cycle approach is embedded in the O'Keeffe College ways of working. The school has been the inspiration and model for numerous other schools that have benefited from adopting the systems that O'Keeffe College has developed. What the school is confident about is that they have developed a method of providing students with visible quick wins with their milestones, they have improved the depth and breadth of their leadership, their organisational practices have been continually refined, and the staff is highly motivated to continually seek improvement in their outcomes. The school can celebrate its successes but acknowledges the challenges it is still trying to address. As noted by Hinnant-Crawford (2020), "Addressing wicked problems in complex systems requires an iterative approach and relentless persistence towards the goal" (p. 92).

References

Bendikson, L., Hattie, J., & Robinson, V. M. J. (2011). Assessing the comparative performance of secondary schools. *Journal of Educational Administration, 49*(4), 443–449.

Gray, J., Goldstein, H., & Thomas, S. (2001). Predicting the future: The role of past performance in determining trends in institutional effectiveness at A level. *British Educational Research Journal, 27*(4), 391–405.

Hinnant-Crawford, B. N. (2020). *Improvement science in education: A primer.* Myers Education Press.

Little, J. W. (2002). Professional community and the problem of high school reform. *International Journal of Educational Research, 37*, 693–714.

Locke, E. A., & Latham, G. P. (2013). Goal setting theory, 1990. In E. A. Locke & G. P. Latham (Eds.), *New developments in goal setting and task performance* (pp. 3–15). Routledge.

Thomas, S., Peng, W. J., & Gray, J. (2007). Modelling patterns of improvement over time: Value added trends in English secondary school performance across ten cohorts. *Oxford Review of Education, 33*(3), 261–295.

CHAPTER FOUR

Defining the Problem
and the Goal

In this chapter, we explain why it is important to clearly define a problem and articulate what an effective goal entails, and how to set a measurable target related to the goal. We give examples of how a primary and a secondary school defined their priority problems and determined their initial goals.

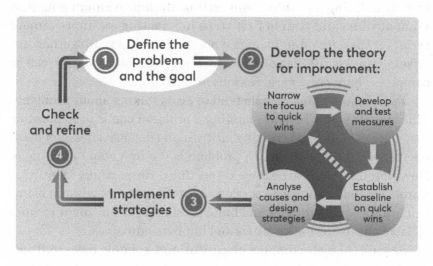

Figure 4.1. The School Improvement Cycle: Define the Problem and the Goal

Why Define a Problem?

Many people react negatively to the idea of defining a problem. They talk instead of opportunities or strength-based approaches. While schools should always build on their strengths, they are not motivated to improve if they do not see something as problematic. Only if people see elements of the status quo as problematic are they willing to act to address them. They can then start to understand and define the problem and pursue an improvement goal linked to that problem.

Spending time clearly and accurately defining the problem is important, because an inaccurate definition will lead to a lack of clarity in the later steps. Without this clarity, one might attempt to solve a problem that does not exist, measure outcomes not linked to the problem, or put strategies in place that do not address the causes of the problem. If the linkage is missing between the problem and the strategies to monitor and address it, little improvement will be made.

Why Is It Difficult to Define a Problem?

Clearly defining a problem and setting an improvement goal may seem obvious and simple first steps in enacting an improvement cycle, yet they are often managed poorly. That is not altogether surprising, because the idea of clearly defining a problem to solve can be complex. There are several reasons for this.

First, as just noted, people tend to avoid talking about problems. This may be partly because naming a problem can lead to pointing the finger of blame and creating mistrust and defensiveness, yet being open about the existence of a problem is the first step to solving it. However, this needs to be done respectfully. Respectfully identifying a problem and inviting a discussion about the evidence without blame can bring people together and build trust and commitment to work collaboratively to resolve issues and improve outcomes.

Second, like all complex organisations, schools have multiple problems and areas for improvement such as for people, property, finances, community engagement, teacher development, and student outcomes. Leaders need to deal with them all, and to some degree, all at once. The dilemma for school leaders becomes: "How do I solve all these problems?" or "How do I focus on school improvement when I have all these other responsibilities?" Focusing on multiple problems dilutes the focus and often ends in too many strategies being pursued and in teachers and students being overwhelmed with what is sometimes referred to as *initiative-itis*. Further, if schools do get an improvement, they are often unable to articulate how they achieved that improvement. They have no way of discerning the discrete effect of the multiple actions they have taken.

Third, it can be challenging for schools to distinguish between "the problem" and "the causes of the problem". For example, is the problem low levels of skills in students, a lack of good teaching of those same skills, or a lack of leadership to promote the teaching of those skills?

The answer to these dilemmas is to focus on one student-centred priority problem at a time. A student-centred problem is focused on the outcomes that the students are attaining—not on what the adults need to do. Improving student outcomes should be the priority for schools, and evidence suggests that the stronger the focus on student outcomes, the greater the gain for students (e.g., Robinson et al., 2008). This is particularly notable in schools that serve low-income communities. Some schools stand out as highly successful in these communities despite the challenges that their students might be experiencing outside of school (e.g., Chenoweth, 2007) because their approach to improvement is unrelenting and focuses on increasing the opportunities for students to learn by ensuring that all students spend more time on worthwhile learning tasks; the approach is constantly driven by active and ongoing monitoring of academic data (Hattie, 2012). Schools should not solely focus on academic outcomes; however, enabling their students to achieve academically should be a school's priority because not many schools can say that they do not have some issues with the quality or the equity of their academic results. For example, how many secondary schools can say they are achieving optimal results for all students and cannot possibly improve them? And how many primary schools can say that they have almost every student performing at their age-appropriate level in literacy and numeracy? Thus, with the plethora of potential problems that any school could start with, we strongly recommend that analysing academic data is the best starting point to identify a problem for an initial improvement cycle.

The student-centred priority problem becomes the basis for setting an initial improvement goal and designing strategies for improvement. The problem, and the associated goal, drive the school's teacher development agenda. Teacher learning goals become a strategy for reaching the student-centred improvement goal; they are not separate or additional goals. They are derived from what teachers need to learn to improve quick-win outcomes. Any accountability about teacher learning or development can be attested to by the quick-win data teachers collect. Therefore, there is no need for a separate teacher "appraisal system"; the data are gathered by carrying out the quick wins in teams as part of their business-as-usual practice. No time-wasting through separate meetings or observations is required. All the "accountability" can be achieved simply by executing improvement cycles.

Thus, focusing on a specific student-achievement problem and its associated goal through an improvement cycle tends to drive other decisions. In short, being strategic by implementing improvement cycles focused on student outcomes simplifies managing a complex environment and reduces the number of goals for teachers and leaders. With this scenario, leaders still must pursue their property, finance, and health and safety goals, but the teachers need to focus on only one or, at the most, two goals. And leaders' approach to leading improvement becomes a routine where everyone knows how the cycles work and do their part in creating and following through with them.

From a Priority Student-centred Problem to a Goal and a Target

Teachers, students, and parents would likely all identify different priority problems to solve. To negotiate this complexity, we recommend that the first step in identifying a problem is to review historical academic results. Numerous data sources may be considered, such as results from local assessments, standardised tests, and the qualification data of school leavers. Analysing the school's academic performance patterns over time is the most useful place to start to decide on an initial problem to solve.

Other quantitative and qualitative data tend to add to the analysis of the academic data but can wait until later. For example, a review of student attendance and retention data may help to highlight potential causes of problems with the academic data. If there are high absentee rates, that may be a cause of low achievement. If there is poor retention of students in one year and high attainment results in the cohort the following year at a secondary school, it may indicate that the "harder to teach" students have left, not that the school has become more effective. Similarly, attitudinal data may add to people's theorising about the causes of the problem. For example, if students are not feeling challenged, that may be contributing to underperformance. These analyses are important, but come later.

Many schools nowadays have access to such a wide range of academic data that reviewing it can seem overwhelming. While some level of data literacy is undoubtedly useful, a school does not have to have a statistician to do this work. The following section sets out the core steps to approach the analysis. To increase clarity for the reader, we have set out the steps in deciding on the priority problem, goal, and target in the following manner: narrow down the data set; identify the high-level limiting factor; articulate clearly the high-level problem; articulate the high-level goal; disaggregate the data; refine the goal; and set a measurable target.

Narrow Down the Data Set

The first step is to scan historical data on academic achievement. Historical data include student achievement data from the last 3 to 5 years—or even further in the past if the data are accessible. The data should be in a comparable format, which is sometimes hindered by changes in schools' reporting, reporting systems, or types of assessments. When that occurs, leaders should decide on the results they most value and accept that they may only have comparable patterns for 1 or 2 years. So long as they adhere to using the same assessments and format of displaying data in the future, analysing trends will become easier as each year passes. Many schools are fortunate to have data collated and presented to them by their educational system leaders. If there are a lot of data, leaders need to decide what to focus on. Too much data can be overwhelming and lead to a lack of fruitful analysis.

In examining the data, deciding what indicators are the most important in the school context is important. What are the results the school values knowing about? For example, most primary schools closely examine their mathematics, reading, and writing results. Most secondary schools review their qualification data. This is because these results are usually highly valued and available to be presented in a standardised form.

Thus, school leaders should narrow down their high-level historical data to those results that they really value and want to monitor closely year after year. They do this by compiling a *data overview* document so that any obvious patterns can be readily discerned and discussed. In a New Zealand secondary school, this would be a historical overview of the NCEA data. Fortunately, the government provides this to schools. In Australian schools, this would be NAPLAN (National Assessment Program—Literacy and Numeracy) data and qualification data such as HSC (Higher School Certificate). In a primary school, this would be an overview of the reading, writing, and mathematics results over the years, preferably from standardised assessments if available. Standardised tests such as Progressive Achievement Tests (PATs) are a common source of these lag indicators. It is these long-term patterns that help school leaders to prioritise an initial, high-level problem.

Table 4.1 illustrates how a primary school might collate that data to keep an eye on the overall trends in subjects indicating the percentage of students achieving at or above the standard generally expected for that age group, and then break each subject down to look at the trends for different ethnic groups (Table 4.2), genders (Table 4.3), and cohorts of students (Table 4.4) in each subject. In Table 4.2, the numbers of Pacific students are very small, so they are denoted with an asterisk and footnote indicating that numbers less than 10 students will not be publicly reported. Schools often keep the number and the percentage evident in their tables by putting the number in parentheses within the cell. Keeping tables such as these and adding to the data every year makes the patterns very easy to graph and allows for an ongoing review without much effort.

Table 4.1. Percentage of Students Achieving at or Above the Standard

Subject Area	2015	2016	2017	2018	2019
Reading	81	85	86	93	95
Written Language	76	76	76	92	90
Mathematics	77	80	84	90	91

Table 4.2. Percentage of Main Ethnic Groups Achieving at or Above the Standard

Ethnic Group	2015	2016	2017	2018	2019
Māori	76	80	66	78	80
Pacific	72	85	*	*	*
Asian	82	76	77	84	87
European	76	76	76	82	80

* Numbers below 10

Table 4.3. Percentage of Male and Female Students Achieving at or Above the Standard

Gender	2015	2016	2017	2018	2019
Male	72	65	68	89	88
Female	81	89	84	95	93

Table 4.4. Percentage of Cohorts Year on Year Achieving at or Above the Standard

Year Level	2015	2016	2017	2018	2019
Year 2	93	86	99	97	96
Year 3	68	76	96	92	91
Year 4	83	78	95	88	87
Year 5	71	78	87	91	87
Year 6	66	62	91	83	93

Australia's NAPLAN provides a rich array of options for reviewing results. A table such as Table 4.5 may help leaders to discern their priority area of concern. It helps leaders assess their progress over the eight previous years. The same can be done for the last two years to see if the school's results are trending positively or not.

Most importantly, schools should assess how they are performing compared to similar schools. The comparison to similar schools reveals the degree to which a school adds value, because it considers the differing socioeconomic effects on schools. For example, if a school is already relatively high-performing, it may have to work hard to maintain those levels, whereas if a school is relatively under-performing, there is room for improvement. In Table 4.5, a school may decide that focusing on mathematics is the next priority problem to solve because the school is underperforming compared to similar schools, and performance has been regressing.

Table 4.5. NAPLAN Patterns of Achievement Over Time

Subject Area	Over eight years	Over last two years	Compared to similar schools now
Y3 Spelling	Maintaining	Improving	Under-performing
Y5 Spelling	Maintaining	Maintaining	Similar
Y3 Writing	Improving	Improving	Exceeding
Y5 Writing	Improving	Improving	Exceeding
Y3 Maths	Maintaining	Regressing	Under-performing
Y5 Maths	Regressing	Maintaining	Under-performing

One particularly useful form of data that NAPLAN provides is the data indicating how different student groups improved between two consecutive NAPLAN tests in a given domain, such as numeracy (see Figure 4.2). These types of graphics give staff a clear picture of how a school is performing compared to schools serving students with the same starting score and a similar background. If a school is under-performing in one area but performing reasonably well in others, that can help a school to determine its priority goal to focus on.

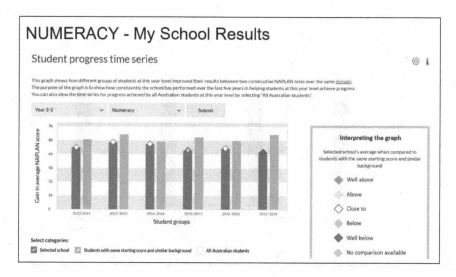

Figure 4.2. NAPLAN Graphic Showing Two Consecutive Tests for a Cohort Compared to Similar Schools

For a secondary school, we advocate keeping an ongoing record of how each department performs compared to similar schools (see Table 4.6) and tracking percentages of all students achieving qualifications. A graph (see Figure 4.3) clearly shows how a school performs department by department compared to similar schools. In these examples, results are reported in bands indicating groups of scores from *low* (bands 1 and 2) to *high* to provide an overview.

Aside from academic outcome data, secondary schools may also find it helpful to track retention data for cohorts in their data overview document, such as in Table 4.7, as these patterns will inform the theorising about causes. Retention from one year to the next is a

Table 4.6. Percentage of Students in HSC (Higher School Certificate) Bands by Department Compared to Similar Schools

Bands	Maths School A	Maths Similar schools	Science School A	Science Similar schools
Bands 1–2	10	8	15	8
Bands 3–4	65	70	75	72
Bands 5–6	35	22	0	20

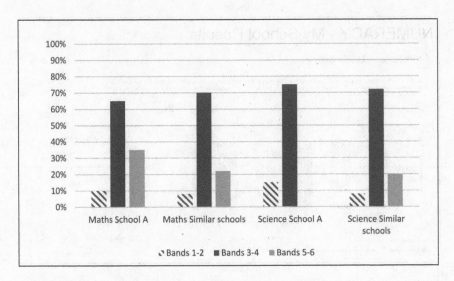

Figure 4.3. Percentage of Students in HSC Bands by Department Compared to Similar Schools

particularly important statistic for secondary schools, as results could look better than they actually are—for instance, they might reflect improvement because struggling students left the school.

Table 4.7. Tracking Student Numbers by Cohort

Year Level	2018	2019	2020	2021	2022	2023
Year 9	300	320	315	340	320	340
Year 10	310	312	314	333	325	335
Year 11	299	301	316	320	320	310
Year 12	265	255	270	275	275	285
Year 13	155	167	185	156	198	202

Attendance is also a critical indicator to track. For example, if attendance has dropped at the same time as the results, that may indicate a causal factor that needs to be addressed. Most schools have some sort of system that they feed into to track attendance, but these data should be converted into easy-to-understand tables in the school's data overview document. This may be the percentage of students attending 95% or more of the time, the percentage attending 85–94%, and so on. While schools typically have data on the average number of days students attend school, it can be helpful to report the percentage of students attending above a threshold because a school can then set clear targets about groups of students whose attendance does not meet that threshold. For example, if 30% of students attend from 75% to 85% of the time, they might be a group that the school could target to improve attendance and, as a result, improve academic outcomes.

Some schools also have good (and simple) ways to track school climate—for example, standardised measures created by external organisations (e.g., a school climate survey) that indicate student, staff, and parent feedback on different aspects of school climate. Anything that is part of a school's theorising about why they are getting specific results should be tracked and the data added to year-on-year in the overview document. With school climate data, it is often useful to pinpoint where the school's results differ from those of the wider population, and try to address and track one or two of those indicators that the school is most concerned about over time.

Identify the High-Level Limiting Factor

Data need to be recorded in tables so they can be added to year-by-year. By doing this, the high-level limiting factor, which is the subject area or qualification result most needing improvement, can be highlighted and then addressed. The data overview allows a school to review the overall patterns and decide on their current priority on an annual basis. The idea of low or poor performance or inadequate student growth may be somewhat subjective in a school. A sound way of making a judgment is to compare results to similar schools in terms of the socioeconomic setting of the school and the ethnic makeup of the student body. Or the judgment may simply be made that a level of performance is not good enough just at face value. For example, when 50% of students drop out without a qualification, regardless of the socioeconomic setting, most people would judge that to be an unacceptable level of school performance. When a school is relatively high-performing but serves a high socioeconomic community, the school may still be underperforming in one subject area or in comparison to similar schools. Every school has room to improve.

Clearly Articulate the High-Level Problem

An appropriate problem is the achievement outcome that most concerns a school or is most limiting for their students at the time. Having identified the problem, it should be straightforward to present that data to staff to see if they agree that it is, indeed, the high-level priority problem to solve. It is critical to present the problem and not just the suggested goal. Staff must be able to see a clear rationale for the goal if they are to be committed to it. First, however, leaders must be able to clearly articulate, "What is the problem we are trying to solve?"

Articulate the High-Level Goal

The goal is the inverse of the problem. For example, if the high-level problem is poor reading comprehension results, the goal is "*To improve reading comprehension*". Once the data showing relatively poor performance in a given area are shared with staff, and it is agreed that this is indeed the problem to be solved, the goal needs to be clearly articulated. This means that the goal should be simple and easy to remember. Everyone can remember that their goal is "*To improve reading comprehension*", but not everyone will remember if there are multiple goals. If goals are not known, they are unlikely to be actively pursued (Bendikson et al., 2020). Use words such as *improve, increase,* and *decrease* as starting verbs to be clear about what the goal is and express it in a short sentence. Everyone in the school should be clear on the goal and be able to recite what it is without having to think about it.

Disaggregate the Data

The next step is to understand where exactly the problem lies and to narrow down the goal focus. Schools need to examine the data by gender (see Table 4.3), ethnicity (see Table 4.2), and interest groups such as learners with English as a second language or new immigrants, to ascertain if results are equitable (or if they are becoming more or less equitable) so that the nature of the problem is better understood. This analysis may point to a more specific area of need due to inequity in results.

Again, beware of small numbers of students within a group being presented in percentages. The smaller the numbers, the less useful percentages are. For example, when a school has a minority group (e.g., an ethnic group with only a small number of students), it is important to monitor the group closely, because they are a minority group and equitable outcomes are desired. But suppose the numbers vary—for example, if there are 10 minority students in the school one year, 15 the next, and 8 the next. In that case, it is not very helpful to show their results in percentages, because this can mislead the viewer of the graph to think that changes from one year to the next are much more extreme than they actually are.

Refine the Goal

After examination of patterns in the disaggregated data, the goal may need to be refined further. The disaggregated data may point to inequities in results by gender or ethnicity. That does not mean that the goal needs to focus only on one gender or one specific ethnic group. Still, it may mean that a school wants to focus particularly on that group while also attending to any other underperforming students. Academic goals should promote equity of outcomes. Thus, a goal such as "*Improve written language*" might be refined to a more specific goal such as "*Improve written language results, particularly for boys*".

Characteristics of a Good Goal

A goal sets the broad direction of improvement. A target specifies a measure and sets a timeframe for it. While targets are key to measuring progress, teachers do not necessarily have to be able to recite the target, but they need to be crystal clear about the goal if they are to be really engaged in achieving it. A good goal motivates staff, is clear, is focused on the students, and is likely to impact a significant group of students. It must also be able to inspire middle leaders and teachers because they are the people who are relied upon to do the work with students. These characteristics are now explained.

Few and Clear

Goals can only be motivational if the team that is expected to enact them is clear on what they are supposed to be pursuing. Thus, straightforward language is important in conveying the goals (e.g., *"Improve reading comprehension"*). When goals are complex, they are unmemorable and therefore demotivating. For example, a goal such as *"All students who have been at the school for three years or more, and who have previously passed their literacy requirements, will attain the Level 1 qualification"* contains too much detail to be memorable and easily translatable in practice. When people formulate complicated goals, they usually try to increase their chances of success by eliminating some students from the goal. However, goals are high-level, broad direction-setters that need to be clear and simple, so they are motivating. Having only one or two student-centred goals is critical because the whole point of goals is to set a priority.

Student-Focused, Not Adult-Focused

There is a tendency for schools to focus their improvement goal on the adults instead of students, which is one of the reasons for starting with student academic data. It gets the focus firmly on the students. We commonly see schools create goals like: *"Improve teacher use of formative assessment"*. These are adult actions or strategies that may help realise student-centred goals and should not be considered as goals. For example, the goal may be *"To improve reading comprehension"*, and one of the strategies might be *"To improve formative assessment in comprehension"*. A strategy is something adults do to reach the school's student-centred goal.

Likely to Impact a Significant Group of Students

There is little point in setting a goal and target to improve something that is not a limiting factor for a significant group of students. The goal and the annual target must focus on a problem that impacts many students if it is to be worth pursuing.

Able to Inspire the Commitment of Most Middle Leaders

In larger schools, middle leaders, such as heads of departments or deans or team leaders, play critical roles in goal pursuit, so their commitment to the goal is the key to success (Locke & Latham, 1990). Middle leaders tend to be the ones with the direct oversight of groups of teachers. Therefore, if they are not committed to the goal, they are unlikely to inspire their teachers to be committed. If the goal is supported in data and the middle leaders have been involved with the decision about the goal, the likelihood of their commitment is enhanced. The perceived validity of the goal is one of the biggest factors in attaining middle leader and teacher buy-in. Another is the competency that the senior leadership team displays in planning and coordinating the improvement strategies that are linked to the goal. If the leaders do not follow through and clearly drive improvement, middle leaders and staff can become cynical and, justifiably, disengage from the improvement process (Bendikson et al., 2020). In small schools, of course, the buy-in of the teachers themselves is key. When there is no team leader, every person's commitment becomes critical.

Other Types of Goals

While primary schools tend to focus on the "basics" of reading, written language, and mathematics, and secondary schools tend to focus on qualification results, schools need to measure the outcomes they truly value. A school does not have to limit itself to goals focused on academic achievement. There may be a good reason to focus on attitudes, competencies, or dispositions. Claxton (2018) depicts three types of learning in "the learning river": knowledge at the top layer, skills and literacies in the next layer, and attitudes and dispositions in the deepest layer.

> Although positive attitudes toward learning lead to better school achievement, we cultivate those attitudes because they are valuable outcomes of education in their own right. That said, concerns with knowledge, literacy, and good grades are entirely compatible with the deliberate cultivation of learning dispositions. These different ends do not have to compete with or disrupt each other. (Claxton, 2018, p. 46)

As Claxton argued, growth in attitudes and competencies are worth pursuing in their own right, and how to measure them is explained in Chapter Seven. However, we strongly recommend that, when measuring progress in these areas, the results are tethered to progress in a curriculum area or qualification. In that way, the theory that improving attitudes or competencies positively affects academic outcomes is tested.

Characteristics of a Measurable Target

Goals broadly indicate the direction of the improvement. These goals need to be detailed in a target. Targets are also known as SMART goals, with the acronym referring to specific, measurable, achievable but challenging, relevant, and time-bound. The meaning of these terms is spelled out below.

Specific

A target is precise about the measure of success. That requires the school leaders to know their *baseline* on an assessment against which progress can be measured. For example, if a school has 65% of its students meeting a certain standard, the baseline is 65%, and its first target might be to improve that to 80%. The degree of performance being sought is clear.

Measurable

This feature, along with *time-bound*, tends to be the most powerful quality of a target because it is the measurement of progress towards a goal that provides feedback to those pursuing it. It allows people to ask questions such as: "How close are we? What more can we do to reach it? Did we reach it or not?" Reaching a target, or coming close to it, because of a focused effort motivates staff to pursue another target or apply strategies to achieve it.

Achievable but Challenging

Targets motivate people if they are really challenging and yet possible to meet with hard and focused work. Suppose the target is close to the result that is already being attained. In that case, a person tends to think, "Well, we are nearly achieving that now", and is therefore not motivated to change their strategy and raise energy levels to actively pursue the new target. On the other hand, if the target is patently out of reach regardless of strategy and effort, a person is likely to be demotivated because they think, "That's impossible, so why try?". A good target is scary because it is a real stretch, yet it might be possible to meet it with a focused strategy and hard work. Even if a school is not successful in reaching the target, just the fact that it pursued a high target will probably mean that it will get close to the target and exceed the achievement it would otherwise have reached without a target (Locke & Latham, 1990).

Relevant

A target needs to be relevant to staff and students. It needs to focus on a priority problem impacting many students to motivate staff to reach the target. Staff must feel committed to the goal if it is to be achieved, because success inevitably requires focused work.

Time-bound

If there is no date by which a target needs to be achieved, it loses its specificity. A looming deadline promotes action and the urge to do more to attain the target. Schools often set an annual target, meaning a long timeframe exists to meet the target. To create urgency, schools must keep communicating about their target and use the quick-win measures to show progress towards it to keep staff and students engaged and committed.

Setting a Measurable Target

There are three main ways of setting targets. The first we call "Finger in the Air" and is most common, the second uses a benchmark set by others, and the third uses real faces and names of students.

Finger in the Air

This is what many schools do. They just pull a number out of the air, such as "Let's go for a 20% improvement", and in practice, this is often very effective if the target meets the condition of being achievable but challenging.

Benchmark

This method uses the performance of other similar schools to set the target, or an externally set target, such as a government-made target. For example, a school could aim to match the performance of schools that are similar to them, exceed the average achievement of the state or country if they are way below that mark, or meet a government-made target.

Real Faces and Names

This method uses a particular benchmark and identifies all the students not reaching that benchmark. This means that rather than setting a percentage target, the school specifies the number of students they want to see achieve. For example, if 240/300 students are performing at an acceptable level, 60 students are underperforming. The achievable but challenging target might be to get another 40 of the 60 currently underperforming students to reach that benchmark, or whatever number is challenging but attainable. Thus, the target would be to get 280/300 to meet the achievement benchmark. The school might arrive at 40 out of 60 as being reasonable from their knowledge of the students. For example, a few students might have specific needs, which means the achievement level would not be realistic for them, or some may have just arrived from another country and still be learning the language. However, while the target should be achievable, it should also be challenging. The school would know the students who are underperforming by name, put action plans for each of the 60 students in place, and track their progress individually. This is an example of the *target-student* approach to improvement cycles. Next, we outline two case studies, one from a primary and one from a secondary school, to illustrate the points made about the goal and target-setting process.

Bonnard Primary School's Goal Setting

Bonnard Primary is an urban, co-educational school with approximately 450 students. It serves a medium-to-high socioeconomic community with a high proportion of migrants. A third of the students have English as a second language.

Narrow Down the Data Set

Like most primary schools, Bonnard Primary tracked its annual results in reading, written language, and mathematics. They have data on other subjects, but they do not have any results from standardised assessments in these other subjects. Because data from non-standardised assessments are less reliable, and literacy and numeracy are viewed as the core learning areas for primary schools, the principal and senior leaders prioritised these subject areas and tracked and examined them each year.

Identify the High-Level Limiting Factor

When the new principal started at Bonnard Primary School, she initially reviewed the high-level historical data from the last 3 years. By *high level*, we mean data that show the percentage of students achieving at the expected levels on annual lag data. It is not examined in depth at this stage. The data that Bonnard Primary's principal reviewed from the previous 3 years is set out in Table 4.8. The data showed relatively poor performance in written language compared to the other core subjects. Mathematics was improving steadily over time, and reading achievement was holding at a steady and high level.

Table 4.8. Historical Overview of Bonnard Elementary's Key Results

Learning area	Percentage of students meeting the expected standard		
	3 years ago	2 years ago	Last year
Reading	81%	85%	86%
Written language	76%	76%	76%
Mathematics	77%	80%	84%

Clearly Articulate the High-Level Problem

This led the new principal to think that the initial problem to solve was performance in written language. On sharing those views with teachers, they were unimpressed. They had been "doing written language" for several years without any discernible improvement. The teachers attributed this lack of progress to the steady stream of new immigrants with low levels of English and therefore low written language skills in English, impacting results.

The principal considered staff feedback, but she was aware that in her last school, which was a school in a similar socioeconomic setting, the written language results were markedly better than in this school. She investigated data from neighbouring schools to see if they had results similar to those of her new school. At the next staff meeting, the principal presented data that compared their high-level written language results to those of a similar, neighbouring school. The difference was marked. Bonnard Primary's results were 14% lower. Some staff described this presentation as a "wake-up call", and staff accepted that their results were not as good as they could be. Nevertheless, staff still pushed back, arguing that the real priority problem in the school was student behaviour. There was a lot of disruption to classroom learning from students with behavioural issues. The principal realised that addressing the issue of student behaviour could not wait if progress were to be made in academic learning. It was demoralising staff and disrupting the opportunities for all students to learn. The school did not have hard data on the size and nature of the problem initially, so this had to be collected.

Articulate the High-Level Goal

The principal knew she had to deal with the disruption as a priority, as a disorderly environment impedes effective teaching and learning and demoralises staff. However, she also felt a sense of urgency to address the priority academic problem. Therefore, after discussion with staff, she proposed two high-level goals: *"Improve classroom behaviour"* and *"Improve written language"*.

Disaggregate the Data

The principal disaggregated the written language data by ethnicity and gender. This step was carried out to illuminate the nature of the problem and, therefore, the nature of the goal upon which the school needed to concentrate. The differences in results between ethnic groups were not profound, but when the principal compared the data of male and female students in written language, a significant gap was evident (see Table 4.9). The principal converted the data from Table 4.9 into a graph (see Figure 4.4) so that staff could see the disparity between male and female results without having to compare numbers. Furthermore, the trend lines on the graph highlighted that boys' results were deteriorating while those of girls were improving. Thus, the gap was increasing over time.

Table 4.9. Historical Overview of Bonnard Elementary School's Data
Disaggregated by Gender

Gender	Percentage of students meeting the expected standard		
	3 years ago	2 years ago	Last year
Male	72%	65%	68%
Female	81%	89%	84%

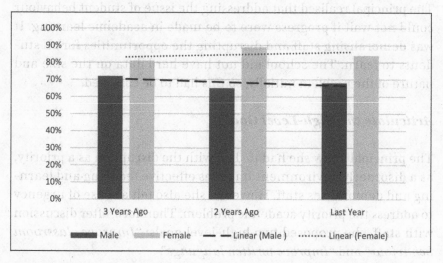

Figure 4.4. Historical Overview of Bonnard Elementary School's Data
Disaggregated by Gender

The importance of graphing data at this stage cannot be overempha-
sised. Graphs, particularly bar graphs, are a prime school improvement tool. They help us to "see" the problem more clearly than by
looking at a table and, thereby, help to enhance staff commitment to
solving it.

Given that the school did not have any data on behavioural issues,
they had to gather baseline data on what issues were occurring, when
they were occurring, what the likely triggers for them were, and
which students were exhibiting these behaviours. Once the school
had baseline data, the school leaders could better understand the
problem. Thus, they initially had teachers gather data on the highly
disruptive behaviour (who, when, what behaviour, possible triggers)
for four weeks.

Refine the Goal

Based on the analysis of the written language data, the school refined their goal from *"Improve written language"* to *"Improve written language, particularly of boys"*. Given that eliminating disruptive behaviour in the classroom was key to improving academic outcomes, the goal to reduce disruptive behaviour was refined to *"Reduce disruptive behaviour in the classroom"*. Other areas or times where disruptive behaviour could occur were left to focus on later. Thus, the goals were refined to be more specific to reflect for whom and when the problematic performance or behaviour was evident.

Set a Target

Recently, 76% of Bonnard Primary students were performing at appropriate levels in written language. However, a school nearby that served a similar student population was attaining 90%. On that basis, Bonnard Primary set a 90% achievement target for all students and aimed for equity in results between boys and girls. Staff perceived this target to be very challenging to achieve but, because it was based on a similar school's performance, it was accepted as attainable, though possibly not in one year.

In relation to the goal *"To reduce disruptive behaviour in the classroom"*, the school used the collected baseline data to set a specific numerical target for reducing the incident rate of disruptive behaviour. Their data over one month showed, on average, 23 major behavioural incidents per week. The school set an initial target to reduce this number to 10 incidents per week. The school engaged a psychologist to assist them in this process and to develop strategies to reduce the disruptions.

Some Lessons from Bonnard Primary

Bonnard Primary settled on two goals in the first year of the new principal's tenure. Two student-centred goals are the maximum we recommend. Severe behavioural disruptions to teaching cannot be ignored. The problem must be addressed because, in the absence of an orderly environment, other improvement efforts are unlikely to be successful (Robinson, 2011). In the meantime, the principal saw the pattern of poor written language results. She felt that that problem could not be ignored either, and made her case to teachers. While teachers were not initially enthusiastic about the written language goal focus, the joint focus helped build some trust as teachers quickly saw a reduction in disruptions. Further, the process for improving behaviour was the same as the improvement cycle process for improving written language, which builds teacher confidence with the improvement cycle approach.

The school focused on the written language goal for two years to close the gap in results by gender and to reach their final desired target of 90%. The behavioural goal was also maintained for 2 years. During that time, the school's expectations on behaviour were raised. Minor disruptions were tracked and addressed the same way as major disruptions had been, and the scope was extended from the classroom to the playground. The school now has a calm and orderly environment, and improving student performance in mathematics is the new priority goal. Still, the school continues to work hard to maintain their levels of performance in written language and to prevent the gender gap in results from opening up again.

Monet College's Goal Setting

Monet College is a co-educational secondary school with approximately 600 students serving a low socioeconomic community in a small, provincial city in New Zealand. About 50% of students are Māori, 30% are European, and the remainder are from diverse ethnic groups.

Narrow Down the Data Set

A comprehensive report on last year's qualification results is provided to schools at the beginning of each academic year by the national education authorities. This report allows each school to compare its current performance against its historical performance and that of similar schools. Thus, the government essentially narrows down the data set for schools by producing a report highlighting these factors. Most New Zealand secondary schools firstly concentrate on the high-level patterns in qualification results, as illustrated in Table 4.10, which shows the school's results in literacy and numeracy, and Level 1–3 data for Monet College over the 3 years before implementing an improvement cycle approach.

Table 4.10. Historical Overview of Monet College's Key Results in Percentage of Students Attaining the Qualification

Subject Area/ Qualification Level	Year 1	Year 2	Year 3
Literacy	76	74	78
Numeracy	81	76	81
Level 1	63	52	56
Level 2	77	80	77
Level 3	55	56	53

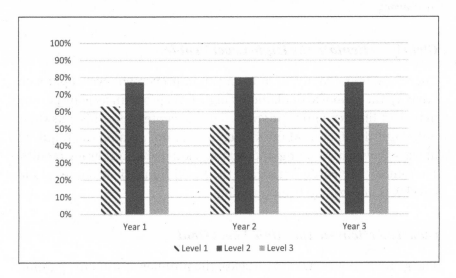

Figure 4.5. Historical Overview of Monet College's Key Qualification Results

Identify the High-Level Limiting Factor

As can be seen in Table 4.10 and Figure 4.5, Monet College's historical performance was relatively stable over the 3 years prior to implementing their first improvement cycles. As the deputy principal stated, "Those were the results we always got, so that was all we thought we could achieve".

Historically, the government had set a target of 85% of 18-year-olds to graduate high school with a Level 2 qualification, so it became common for schools to use this target. Thus, in Years 1–3, Monet College focused on improving Level 2 results; however, their results remained largely unchanged.

Two factors became clear when the college examined their data with an improvement cycle approach, initially focusing on understanding the nature of the problem. First, only about 50–60% of students passed Level 1, meaning many students left school after Level 1. Second, when literacy and numeracy results were examined, the data showed that almost a quarter of the students who sat Level 1 did not pass their literacy credits, and about 20% did not pass numeracy, meaning they could not attain a Level 1 qualification or any other qualification. Thus, the high-level limiting factors were literacy and numeracy.

Clearly Articulate the High-Level Problem

Therefore, in the first year of trying an improvement cycle approach (Year 4), the school articulated its high-level problem as poor performance in literacy and numeracy. They accepted that this was their initial limiting factor. Many students were not gaining the required literacy (covering reading and writing skills) and numeracy credits. Therefore, they could not attain the Level 1 qualification, let alone Level 2, that they had been targeting.

Clearly Articulate the High-Level Goal

The goal, therefore, was to increase the number of students gaining their literacy and numeracy credits. The school set a target of 100%

of students attaining the literacy and numeracy benchmark. While this was aspirational, given that approximately 78% had attained literacy and about 87% had attained numeracy previously, there was clear evidence from similar schools that a rate of over 90% achievement was achievable. The principal set up a giant-sized graph in the school hall to mark off the progress towards the target across the course of the year. The use of such a graph is a positive motivational strategy that helps to keep the target front of mind for both staff and students. Numeracy was easier to pursue, as it was clear that it was the responsibility of the mathematics department. However, literacy does not sit with any one department in a secondary school. It became a special focus for the Senior Leadership Team.

Disaggregate the Data

Leaders should carefully track the data of ethnic groups typically underserved by the system. Monet College's data showed that Māori students were not achieving at the same rate as European students. This was a clear problem to be solved, as is shown in the data in Table 4.11, which shows their historical Level 2 data disaggregated by the two main ethnic groups.

Table 4.11. Historical Overview of Monet College's Level 2 Results by Ethnic Groups

Level 2 Results	Year 1*	Year 2*	Year 3*
Māori	71%	73%	75%
European	75%	82%	85%

* Years depict consecutive years, not year levels of students.

However, graphing these data makes the disparity much clearer: as Figure 4.6 shows, the disparity was growing over time.

Refine the Goal/Set a Target

While aware of this ethnic disparity in results, the school chose not to focus on Māori students. They refined their goal by identifying every

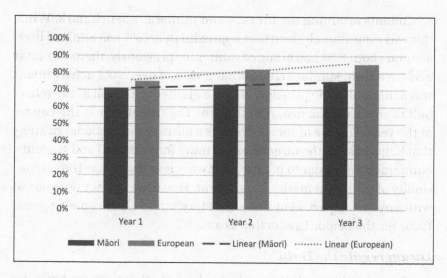

Figure 4.6. Historical Overview of Monet College's Level 2 Results by Ethnic Groups

student by name who had not achieved the literacy or numeracy standard and put plans in place to help each student. Therefore, their approach was a *real faces and names* approach to targeting.

Some Lessons from Monet College

Identifying specific students helped the school improve numeracy results from 81% to 92% and literacy results from 78% to 89% in the first year. Their overall Level 1 results rose by 15%, and the results of Māori students rose by 20%, increasing the equity of results. While the school's Level 1 results rose because of that first year's effort, their Level 2 results dipped in that year (Year 4 in Figure 4.7), as that was not the school's focus. This is not unusual. When a school focuses on one target, results in another area may initially slip. But by the following year (Year 5 in Figure 4.7), having resolved the challenge at Level 1 by successfully focusing on literacy and numeracy and putting in place new systems to sustain those results, Level 2 results also improved as the school applied their improvement methods to Level 2 in the second year of utilising improvement cycles.

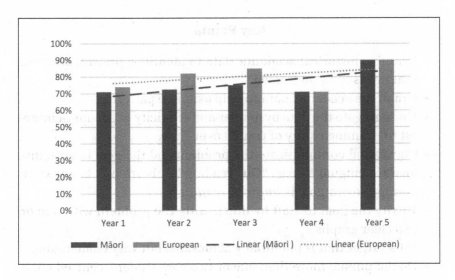

Figure 4.7. Historical Overview of Monet College's Level 2 Results by Ethnic Groups over 5 Years

This case study highlights an important point for all schools. Initial improvement cycle goals should focus on the school's key limiting factor, which is the first major barrier to achievement for most students. In Monet College's case, that involved targeting literacy and numeracy first so that they could raise Level 1 results. Once those were improved, one year later they moved their sights to improving Level 2, and the year after that, to improving Level 3.

Their results improved year-on-year. By Year 6, or the third year of implementing an improvement cycle approach, the school had approximately 93% of students achieving literacy and 99% achieving numeracy. These results were better than those of comparable schools and had a flow-on effect on all their exit qualification data. Level 1 results, 50–60% historically, improved to 84%, and more students were retained. They also saw improvement in Levels 2 and 3. This story speaks to the benefit of being patient and having one good goal and target at a time.

Key Points

- Examine historical academic data to identify a priority problem that needs to be addressed.
- Graph the academic data to help examine patterns.
- Disaggregate the data by gender and ethnicity or groups of interest to examine equity of results over time.
- Clarify and communicate the problem and the goal in straightforward language—e.g., "Our reading levels are way below state average so our goal is *improve reading*".
- Justify the goal to staff by illustrating the problem with one or two clear graphs.
- Set a target that is potentially achievable but very challenging.
- Do not pursue more than one or two core student-centred goals at a time.

References

Bendikson, L., Broadwith, M., Zhu, T., & Meyer, F. (2020). Goal pursuit practices in high schools: Hitting the target? *Journal of Educational Administration*, *58*(6), 713–728.

Chenoweth, K. (2007). *It's being done: Academic success in unexpected schools*. Harvard Education Press.

Claxton, G. (2018). Deep rivers of learning. *Phi Delta Kappan*, *99*(6), 45–48.

Hattie, J. (2012). *Visible learning for teachers: Maximising impact on learning*. Routledge.

Locke, E. A., & Latham, G. P. (1990). *A theory of goal setting and task performance*. Prentice Hall.

Robinson, V. M. J. (2011). *Student-centered leadership*. Jossey-Bass.

Robinson, V. M. J., Lloyd, C., & Rowe, K. J. (2008). The impact of leadership on student outcomes: An analysis of the differential effects of leadership types. *Education Administration Quarterly*, *44*, 635–674.

CHAPTER FIVE

Developing the Theory for Improvement

In this chapter, we provide an overview of the process of developing a theory for improvement, which is also sometimes called a theory *of* improvement. Each individual step is then described in the following chapters. As the diagram below illustrates, we theorise the development of the theory for improvement to be a multi-step process: narrowing the focus to quick wins, developing and testing measures, establishing a baseline on quick wins, analysing the causes of the problem, and identifying the appropriate strategies to address those causes.

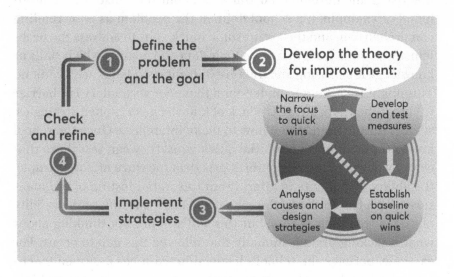

Figure 5.1. The School Improvement Cycle: Develop the Theory for Improvement

This process results in decisions about changes in both pedagogical and organisational practices. Changes are put in place for a period of time, and the efficacy of the changes is tested to see if they indeed resulted in improvement. What is learnt from one cycle is built on in the next. Usually, refinements to improvement strategies are made in each subsequent cycle until the quick-win data indicate that a learning gap has been effectively addressed. In this way, a theory of how to improve results through both pedagogical and organisational changes evolves with each cycle.

While one tends to think of the steps of analysing causes and developing strategies as being at the heart of developing a theory for improvement, in practice we find that it helps schools to start by narrowing down the goal to some initial quick wins that move the school towards the goal, and developing and testing the measures of those quick wins. There are two reasons for this dual focus. First, schools often miss the step of developing measures of quick wins in student learning to address the problem; thus, putting this step first ensures that it is not overlooked. Second, by identifying quick wins and the measures, schools are forced to test the validity of some of their early theorising and develop their thinking about the causes of the problem. For example, if a school defined the problem as poor reading comprehension, and they want some quick wins to address the problem, they would have to turn to their data and analyse which skills or knowledge are missing and thus are impeding students' achievement. This might lead them to understand that poor vocabulary is a barrier to comprehension, but so is a lack of knowledge of explicit strategies, such as how to predict and how to make inferences. Once the school knows these different potential quick wins, they can test these theories by developing a short-term practical measure of, for example, the ability of students to infer. From this initial testing of the measure with a few students, the school will learn a lot about the validity of that part of their theory, but this will also prompt thinking about what is lacking organisationally that allowed this gap to occur. For example, perhaps the school's leadership team has assumed teachers know how to teach comprehension and, as a result, had not laid out adequate guidance and expectations about what needed to be explicitly taught and when. Thus, the development and testing of the first quick-win measures starts a school team on an evidence-based development process of a theory for improvement, as opposed to ad hoc and unfocused brainstorming.

Why Formally Develop a Theory for Improvement?

We all have private theories about why we are getting the results we do. Checking these theories through a formal process serves the purpose of ensuring that a school does not "jump to a pet solution" that is not supported by evidence. Unfortunately, some evidence suggests that leaders are not as analytical as we would like to think. For example, an in-depth study of nine experienced educational leaders (Mintrop & Zumpe, 2019) indicated that leaders tend to define problems in response to a pre-determined solution rather than basing the definition on a rigorous analysis. Even though the leaders were being trained in a problem-solving methodology at the time, most of them focused on a preferred solution that was based on past experience, such as implementing a certain professional development programme (e.g., culturally responsive practices) or a certain practice (e.g., instructional rounds). Choosing what to centre their problem-solving on in their pursuit of school improvement was largely driven by their long-held passions or beliefs about a strategy and not by an analysis of the problem using data about students and student achievement.

Formalising the process of theory development also helps to ensure that a school focuses on sustaining the gains made and does not just focus on short-term gains that may be overridden by future changes. Improvement science is built on a number of fundamental principles, one of which is that "Every system is perfectly designed to get the results it gets". Thus, if a school is experiencing less than satisfactory results, it is not because teachers are not doing their job, or that students are incapable, but rather that the system has not been developed to get better results. That is a leadership issue.

Developing a theory for improvement demands that all elements in the system that maintain an unsatisfactory status quo are examined. These include expectations, documentation, resourcing, teacher knowledge, and, of course, leadership and organisational practices. Improvement does not solely rest on pedagogical improvements. While pursuing agreed pedagogical quick wins can kick-start the process of theory development, wider changes are required to embed the changes coherently in the school's business-as-usual procedures.

How Do You Develop Your Theory?

Making changes and checking for impact is how knowledge about the most effective practice is generated. Cycles of improvement build knowledge through changing practice in iterative cycles until outcomes for diverse groups of students are improved to the desired level. A theory is not adequate if it is only effective for some students. The promotion of equity in outcomes is a key goal of improvement science, and it is achieved by learning in cycle after cycle. "In the context of improvement, a change is a prediction: if the change is made, improvement will result..." (Langley et al., 2009, p. 81).

The improvement cycle methodology constitutes both a deductive and inductive approach to reasoning. Planning and enacting the changes constitutes the deductive approach. This is the prediction or the theory about what will happen if a certain change is made. Then, when carrying out the test of the idea, data are collected and notes are taken about the impact of the idea in comparison to the theorised impact. This is the inductive thinking driven by the data that occurs at the *check and refine* stage: "What happened? What modifications need to be made to the theory or the practice?" To answer these questions, data are required about both the process and the result. To improve written language, for example, this may involve developing a way to judge the effectiveness of a paragraph against criteria (outcome measures), and a way to assess how often and how well the agreed pedagogical strategy was implemented by teachers (process measures). A process measure does not always entail time-intensive observations of all teachers; instead, it could well be a self-report by teachers or observations of a sample of teachers. Thus, every cycle is a process of knowledge development based on theories (deductive) and the testing of that theory with the quick-win data (inductive). If what is learnt is embedded as standard practice, this process results in a continually improving system.

By knowing the improvement cycle's scientific and industrial roots, it is easier to understand that the cycle works because it relies on identifying and amending actions in the workflow to get a better "product". In our case, it is how the school leads teaching and learning to get better student outcomes. This reliance on improving routines and structures is, in many cases, under-valued when strategy is discussed in educational literature. Often, when leaders espouse to be following an improvement cycle, it is only specific adjustments to teaching that are focused on through professional development, and little consideration is given to making amendments in the systems that maintain the way in which teaching occurs. In fact, some argue that the focus of *collective inquiry* (a term sometimes used for implementing improvement cycles) is the promotion of teacher learning (e.g., Donohoo & Velasco, 2016). We disagree. In our view, the purpose of improvement cycles is improving student outcomes; adult learning is a by-product that enables the improvement. This is well illustrated in a health context, where health outcomes are improved not by trying to enhance surgical knowledge and procedures, but by improving the fidelity of the surgical team in using some basic and generic practices to safeguard the patient. Thus, any theory for improvement must not only focus on pedagogical changes that are needed, but also the organisational changes required to underpin and maintain effective pedagogical changes.

Therefore, just as in the health example in Chapter One, the voices of those impacted by the system need to be engaged to develop a valid theory. The teachers' and students' voices need to be heard. To cite a real-life example involving teacher voice, the Senior Leadership Team of one school that was concerned about its written language results theorised that the poor results were, at least partially, due to a lack of explicit teaching. But when the teachers were asked about their theories, one of the main issues that they identified was that students who were most at risk in written language were also performing poorly in reading, and these students were being removed from class for a one-on-one reading intervention (reading recovery) during the same morning sessions as the written language teaching was occurring. In other words, the leaders had theorised about a pedagogical cause for the problem, whereas the teachers theorised about an organisational and leadership cause. The teachers' theory was tested with some timetabling changes so that reading recovery and the teaching of written language did not overlap. The teachers were vindicated in their theory. The students improved faster when they benefited from a double dose of literacy instruction as opposed to sacrificing one session.

No school performance issue is due to one cause. There will always be multiple causes, which is why the perspectives of all key stakeholders need to be engaged with to understand how the system is working in the eyes of different parties and to develop an effective theory for improvement. "A system is an interdependent group of items, people, or processes working together toward a common purpose" (Langley et al., 2009, p. 77). Schools, like other workplaces, are made of multiple systems comprising different teams of people, departmental structures, and resources. Teachers are guided in the way they carry out their work by various levels of leadership and the systems that leaders create. The role of leadership is to optimise outcomes, but their success in this depends on how well they can forge their teams of teachers to work for common goals in co-ordinated ways. To do that, leaders must understand the way teachers are impacted by the current systems or practices.

Students are also part of this process. When adults have theories about the students, they need to test those with the students. Too often, adults have theories about reasons for problems without checking them. Parents can also assist with theory development. One school that achieved very good results overall but had a core group of students performing poorly actively sought input from the students' parents on their views about how the school could better help their child. This approach led to the parents feeling respected and valued and demonstrated to the parents that the teachers cared about their child. The relationships that then developed between these parents and teachers meant that the school and the parents ultimately felt that they had a tailored, collaborative approach with agreed-upon practices that were mutually reinforcing to help support the students.

This story highlights the value of wide "team engagement" in developing a theory for improvement. Engaging with stakeholders is particularly important for effective causal analysis, and it helps build commitment and trust in people's competence to address problems. The improvement cycle is built on the knowledge of the people who work within the system—teachers, students, and parents all experience the current system and are therefore a source of information on potential improvements.

External expert input and access to research can also play a significant role in developing theories for improvement. Schools can bring in researchers or experts in specific areas of need to support the causal analysis. In other situations, a school may be confident about the causes of the problem but not about the potential strategies to address it. This is where the advice of experts or drawing on research can help. For example, one school had solid evidence that students struggled to make inferences from text, but they were not confident on how to best address this gap in a large and complex secondary school. They wanted an approach that any department could use with ease and which was grounded in research. The senior and middle leaders reviewed research literature and found some consensus about the benefits of using an approach that they decided to test. The heads of departments first tested the strategy and the measurement tool they developed with one of their own classes before introducing it to their teams of teachers. They used their experience and results to advocate for the approach that they had found to be both easy to implement and effective. These heads of department had done the initial hard work of researching, trialling, and testing the approach with their own classes. This won them the confidence of their staff when the school scaled up the approach to all classes.

Similarly, schools may investigate how other schools have solved the same problem. One example is a secondary school that had quite pervasive cultural issues that led to low expectations of students and relatively low performance. The leadership team began to develop their theory for improvement based on leader, student, and teacher voice about the nature of the problem and possible responses, but ultimately turned to a school that had resolved similar cultural and performance issues over time for some advice regarding a strategy for addressing these problems.

In summary, a school needs powerful reasons for adopting strategies that they expect will address the various causes of the problem. These strategies can be based on expert advice, from doing their own research on practices that are proven to be effective, or the experience of others in a similar position (Lai et al., 2010).

What Is a Good Theory for Improvement?

The test of a good theory can be summed up in three key factors: the validity of the reasoning; its effectiveness; and its coherence with other systems in the school (Lai et al., 2010). These characteristics make the new learning and the changes in pedagogical and organisational practices likely to be sustained. This was illustrated in Gauguin Primary's approach, described in Chapter Two. The school persisted with their goal for 3 years, by which time the leaders felt that the teachers were driving the process. They noted that teachers would even keep working in the new ways if there were to be a change in leadership.

First, the theory for improvement should be based on verifiable facts, not suppositions. Before adopting solutions, the validity of the underlying thinking about both the causes and the solutions needs to be checked. Often this only requires talking to teachers, students, or parents about causes of problems or the input from research or external experts about the best potential solutions.

Second, the theory's effectiveness is judged by whether or not it works. Does the school ultimately get improved results in their lag data? That is the real test of the effectiveness of the theory. However, if the quick wins have been well chosen and their results show good improvement, then a school should have confidence that the ultimate results in lag data will reflect that success. If the lag data, which is usually collected at the end of the academic year, does not show the hoped-for improvement, either the theory or its enactment was faulty. Yet, while this seems self-evident, we have known schools that have continued to hold fast to a theory for years, despite not getting improved results. These schools tend to claim that "good things take time," and it may take another year or two to see the results. Meanwhile, more and more students are going through the school and failing. It is this problem that the effective use of cycles of improvement should avoid, because the quick wins are the short-term test of strategy effectiveness and, so long as there is also a process measure that provides assurance that the agreed strategy is being implemented by teachers, then the results should be positive.

Third, the systems and practices that are implemented should create greater coherence within a school. For example, one of the greatest risks of any new theory for improvement is that it will lead to greater teacher workload and disenchant rather than motivate teachers. When practices are visibly effective and yet not an imposition on teachers, they will happily sustain the changes that cause visible improvement for their students. By embedding these changed practices into school systems, best practice becomes standard practice. That is the goal: a continually improving school.

Key Points

- It is important to be open and not have pet causes and pet solutions in mind when undertaking an analysis of the problem.
- Formally developing a theory for improvement helps prevent jumping to pet solutions.
- Cycles of improvement build knowledge through iterative cycles of theorising (deductive reasoning) and checking data on quick wins (inductive reasoning).
- Analysis of causes can be supported by engaging experts to review practices or by attaining student, teacher, and parent voice.
- Strategies to address causes can be developed from the advice of experts, insights from research, and other schools that have successfully addressed the same problem.

References

Donohoo, J., & Velasco, M. (2016). *The transformative power of collaborative inquiry: Realizing change in schools and classrooms.* Corwin.

Lai, M., Timperley, H., & McNaughton, S. (2010). Theories for improvement and sustainability. In H. Timperley & J. Parr (Eds.), *Weaving evidence, inquiry and standards to build better schools* (pp. 53–70). NZCER Press.

Langley, G. J., Moen, R. D., Nolan, K. M., Nolan, T. W., Clifford, N. L., & Provost, L. P. (2009). *The improvement guide: A practical approach to enhancing organisational performance* (2nd ed.). Jossey-Bass.

Mintrop, R., & Zumpe, E. (2019). Solving real-life problems of practice and education leaders' school improvement mind-set. *American Journal of Education, 125,* 295–344.

CHAPTER SIX

Narrowing the Focus to Quick Wins

This chapter focuses on quick wins in student outcomes. Quick wins have many names, including *lead indicators*, *small wins*, *intermediate outcomes*, or *just-in-time data*. All terms indicate the nature of these outcomes. This chapter begins with an explanation of the nature of quick wins. We outline two major approaches to quick wins: the *target student* approach and the *common needs* approach. These two approaches are exemplified in the two case studies presented in Chapters Two and Three: Gauguin Primary and O'Keeffe College. We describe how quick wins motivate students and staff, and we illustrate how to identify them.

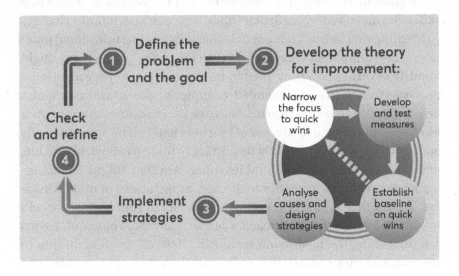

Figure 6.1. The School Improvement Cycle: Narrow the Focus to Quick Wins

What Are Quick Wins?

The technical term for measures of quick wins is *lead indicators*, because they provide an early warning about whether the adopted strategy is working or not. The quick wins are validated by the *lag indicators*, i.e., the data schools typically only attain once a year, such as data from standardised tests. For example, in a secondary school, the successful completion of a number of key tasks or assessments (lead indicators) may be a good predictor of students' ability to pass an end-of-year examination (lag indicator). Thus, quick wins are predictors of future success. Alternatively, and of equal importance, they may reveal to a school, in a timely way, that a strategy is not effective. "The idea is to test fast, fail fast and early, learn and improve" (Bryk et al., 2015, p. 29). If a school team does not see results from their quick-win data, then the teachers can conclude that the strategy they are applying will not be successful in the long term. Thus, the quick-win data provide timely feedback and the opportunity to change the approach. "Absent continuous feedback of such data, one can easily maintain a belief in the efficacy of one's actions even when the warrant for this remains uncertain or non-existent" (Bryk et al., 2015, p. 15).

A student-centred quick win refers to a concept to be learnt or a skill to be mastered by students. Quick wins can also refer to changes to teaching practice or changes to leadership and organisational practices. For example, in carrying out the causal analysis, a team might identify several tasks that need to be carried out, or organisational practices that need to be amended. Completing these tasks might also be considered to be quick wins because their absence represents a roadblock to the future success of teachers and can be systematically addressed. One example could be putting in place a robust, justifiable, and clear plan for professional learning. Another might be changing job descriptions to reinforce the new expectations of middle leaders. Yet another might be creating an artefact to capture the school's learning about how to best teach a certain concept. These quick wins are something the leadership team can "tick off" as contributing to success, and they can occur simultaneously as teachers are testing a pedagogical strategy to attain a quick win on student achievement, or sequentially, with one following the other so that the work is spread between the pedagogical and organisational focus. However, in this book, when we talk about quick wins, we are usually referring to the pedagogical quick wins that teachers implement, which are measured using process data as well as outcome data.

It is important to note that work on quick wins occurs alongside business-as-usual teaching, and indeed, the approach itself becomes business-as-usual. With student-centred quick wins, all teachers on a team agree on the quick-win strategy which, for example, could be a decision to teach a concept for 10 minutes per day to the group of students for whom the quick win was a gap. Then all teachers pursue this strategy in an agreed way. The power of the quick win is derived from its impact on a significant number of students and the importance of the outcome upon which it is focused.

Quick wins are aligned to the longer-term goal that a school is trying to achieve and represent a small step towards that goal. A quick win is "a concrete, complete, implemented outcome of moderate importance" (Weick, 1984, p. 43). Quick wins are not just a random selection of "low-hanging fruit"—that is, things that need doing and can quickly give the appearance of an improvement. They are not learning outcomes that students have almost mastered anyway. Quick wins are a valuable outcome in their own right, and when accumulated, they will ultimately have an impact on the school's longer-term goal.

Two Major Approaches to Quick Wins

There are two approaches that schools commonly take with quick wins: either a *target student* approach, or what we call a *common needs* approach. The target student approach is also sometimes referred to as a *priority student* approach. The idea behind this approach is that teachers first focus on accelerating the learning of a small group of students, but then apply that learning to a wider group of students whom they monitor less frequently or not to the same degree of depth. Target students are typically students who are not achieving at their age-appropriate level in a subject or classroom but have the ability to do so. Teachers often focus on the same target students for numerous cycles, possibly up to a year or longer. They remain target students until they have achieved an age-appropriate level and have shown the ability to maintain the necessary progress without receiving the more intensive teaching. Gauguin Primary School's approach, which was described in Chapter Two, is an example of this method.

Target student groups can be set up in different ways. For example, schools sometimes identify a sample of three to six students who are performing at roughly three different levels (*above, at,* and *below* the age-appropriate level) of achievement. The information arising from monitoring students at different achievement levels provides teachers with feedback on what is working for whom under different conditions, remembering that very able students need to be stretched as much as anyone else. What teachers learn from testing their measurement tool and pedagogical strategy with the target group is applied to all students later.

More commonly, schools establish groups of about six students who are performing below the age-appropriate level of achievement. However, these should not be students identified as having severe learning needs, as those students usually have their own learning programmes and support. Targeting students achieving below expected levels, but with the potential to achieve better, promotes more intensive teaching of students with higher needs but still provides information about the strategy's success at accelerating progress that can be applied to all students.

The benefit of the target student approach is that it enables very close teaching and monitoring of the quick wins of a key group of students from which teachers learn and adjust their teaching. Essentially, if a new teaching practice is effective with this group, it is likely to be effective with the wider group of students in the class. However, the risk is that teachers will not apply what they learn to the wider class. Therefore, it is important to point this out to teachers. The target group is essentially a laboratory where they test theories to improve their effectiveness. Once they see an impact on the target group's performance, they spread the successful teaching practice to the whole-class level.

The alternative approach to monitoring quick wins is a *common needs* approach in which schools monitor achievement of all students using the quick-win measures. This is not difficult or time-consuming when the pre- and post-data are easy to gather. The advantage of this approach is that teachers have detailed data on each student from which decisions can be made about *common needs* within the class. The number of students requiring more in-depth teaching and instruction can then be narrowed down in each subsequent improvement cycle. For example, a school may find that many students are not consistently able to locate information in a text or to make inferences from such information. Further, limited vocabulary is impeding their ability to make inferences. These areas of need may be the first three quick wins for this school. The third area of need, however, would have to be broken down into smaller and more manageable quick wins, perhaps by having teachers decide on some specific vocabulary related to the topic they are currently teaching, or a topic that they want the students to focus on in their own writing.

The teachers may well decide to approach these quick wins one at a time, or, if the outcomes are strongly interrelated, they may want to pursue two or three quick wins at once. As teachers complete each improvement cycle, they would identify the students who still have not mastered the skill focused on as a quick win and examine how they could provide further support and allow the students to develop mastery in the next cycle. Thus, the group of students the teachers start with may be the whole class, or students who have shown a weakness in these skills, but the intense focus of the teachers would move to a smaller and smaller group after each cycle, until all or almost all students have developed mastery of the skills identified as quick wins.

The difference between this approach and the target student approach is that, for each quick win, a different group of target students will be revealed by the data. The *common needs* approach targets key learning outcomes *and* key groups of learners. This approach was exemplified by the O'Keeffe College case study in Chapter Three. The school targeted every student in the school to achieve key outcomes in each subject area.

How Do Quick Wins Impact Goal Achievement?

Once the first quick win is achieved by most of the targeted students, the team of teachers can move onto the next one. Cumulatively, these quick wins help students reach their ultimate goals. Then the quick wins accrue. Staff and students find the visible results in both the short term and the longer term to be rewarding. The accumulation of success builds their collective efficacy. But how one moves from one quick win to the next is not necessarily a tidy, linear process.

> Small wins do not combine in a neat, linear, serial form, with each step being a demonstrable step closer to some pre-determined goal. More common is the circumstance where small wins are scattered and cohere only in the sense that they move in the same general direction or all move away from some deplorable condition. (Weick, 1984, p. 43)

A group of teachers would not move onto a new quick win until almost all students had control of the first one. If the data show that the concept is still not learnt by many students, another improvement cycle would be followed, but it would potentially be one with some different strategies on how to teach the targeted skills, and mainly focused on the group of students who still need to master the quick win. Once most students have mastered the first quick win, the group of teachers would decide to move onto the next one. Any student who had not mastered the first quick win would continue to receive attention until they did. That might not prevent the teacher and student from also working on the next quick win.

Some schools focus on up to four quick wins at a time, but this is often because the concepts overlap. The decision on whether to proceed with quick wins one at a time or a few at a time is best made on the basis of evidence. Does the first cycle show a marked improvement in one of the quick wins, or all of them? If so, what are the implications of that evidence? We recommend one—or maybe two—quick wins at a time as optimal if quick results are to be seen. To illustrate these points more clearly, we now outline characteristics that make quick wins effective as predictors of future success.

Quick Wins Address Limiting Factors

Limiting factors are identified obstacles to future learning; they are "sticking points" for students. If mastered, they help with the next steps in the learning or teaching process, and if not mastered, they impede future learning. For example, if students cannot write an effective paragraph, they cannot write an effective extended text. The knowledge and the skill required to write a paragraph, or lack thereof, impacts students' future learning outcomes. A quick win should focus on addressing these limiting factors.

Quick Wins Impact a Significant Group of Students

If the targeted gap in knowledge or skill affects only a few students, then successfully addressing it is not going to impact the school's overall results. Of course, any gaps for students need to be addressed, but a quick win is a systematic focus across a number of classes, so any nominated quick win needs to be impactful on a large proportion of the students if it is to be worth this effort and focus.

Quick Wins Are Common to a Number of Classes

It will not help a school to improve if every class is pursuing its own quick wins. The power of quick wins is that they drive up coherence and the use of agreed-upon standards of achievement. They can only do that if quick wins are common to several classes across a school. Different groups of teachers, such as junior, middle, and senior teams in a primary school, or different departments in a secondary school, may have different quick wins, but a group of teachers should be addressing some common longer-term goal to have an impact.

Quick Wins Are a Reliable Predictor of the Larger Goal

It is important that quick wins are truly a predictor of success, as indicated by the lag data. The first year that a school works with quick wins is the test of the validity of their quick wins. If staff see progress with their quick wins, and they take the steps to maintain that growth, they should be certain of long-term success.

Quick Wins Are Readily Embedded in the Day-To-Day Work

If quick wins add value for teachers without adding any significant workload, they are likely to succeed. For example, if implementing a strategy for a quick win merely entails all teachers using a certain strategy for a certain period of time in their teaching, this may add no burden whatsoever. Its effectiveness comes from every teacher emphasising the same skill or knowledge gap in a consistent way.

Quick Wins Are Easily Measured

If the measurement tool is too onerous, it will add to teachers' work-load instead of enhancing their work practices. Measuring does not have to be onerous. It may involve noting a skill on a checklist or rubric when it is observed, or it may be achieved by formally assessing a skill orally or in written form. However, if implementing improve-ment cycles is to become "the way we do things around here", mea-surement must be integral to teachers' everyday work. The purpose of the measure is to provide feedback on teaching effectiveness, not to tick a box or create more work.

Quick Wins Are Quick!

The quick win must be a learning outcome that can be achieved quickly. In practice, this often requires 3–5 weeks in a primary school setting, and up to about 10 weeks in secondary schools, where students typically have limited hours per week in a given subject to address a quick win. Meyers and Hitt (2018) cite 30 days as the time to achieve a quick win, while others, such as Hattie (2015) and Timperley and colleagues (2014), suggest starting with a rule of thumb of about 10 weeks and then adjusting the time as needed. However, it should not be longer than 10 weeks, because the whole notion of improvement cycles is one of rapid tests of a change idea. By and large, the shorter the timeframe the better, because feedback on demonstrating some level of mastery has a significant effect on commitment to the goal and, therefore, the effort (Klein et al., 1999). The length of time is a site-by-site decision to be made based on the size of the quick wins and the amount of time teachers have on a given subject. The important thing is that the length of time of a cycle is set before the cycle is enacted, so that all teachers know when their quick-win data are due, and they bring the data together for analysis across the school or group of classes.

How Do Quick Wins Work?

Quick wins play an essential part in the cycle of improvement. Without them, there is no improvement cycle, because there is no feedback mechanism to teachers and students on the effectiveness of their improvement efforts. The feedback promotes motivation in both students and teachers. In Chapter Four, we talked about goals needing to be *clear* and to set a *direction* that people can put *strategic effort* into progressing. Regularly seeing progress from quick-win data motivates more effort, persistence, and strategising to improve results. Visible progress motivates further action and commitment to the goal. And because there is the time and space to concentrate on the goal and see quick progress, people are energised. Amabile and Kramer (2011) refer to it as the *progress principle*:

> Of all the things that can boost emotions, motivation, and perceptions during a workday, the single most important is making progress in meaningful work. And the more frequently people experience that sense of progress, the more likely they are to be creatively productive in the long run. (p. 4)

Thus, quick wins energise and excite people and give them the boost required to keep trying different things to get different results. They make progress both manageable and visible: "A small win reduces importance ('this is no big deal'), reduces demands ('that's all that needs to be done'), and raises perceived skill levels ('I can do at least that')" (Weick, 1984, p. 46).

Quick wins not only impact commitment and motivation; they also impact the collective efficacy of both teachers and students (Bandura, 1993). Collective teacher efficacy is a powerful predictor of success with student outcomes. Collective teacher efficacy is considered by some to be the "number one factor influencing student achievement" (Donohoo, 2017, p. ix). And the greatest driver of self-efficacy is positive short-term feedback through evidence of mastery of a skill. Both students and teachers see that they can be successful, and thus they are motivated to continue to get that positive feedback. One quick win leads to another, and ultimately to enhanced overall student performance and greater teacher satisfaction.

How Are the First Quick Wins Identified?

To identify the initial quick wins, a team needs to gather more specific data on the goal focus or analyse data it already has in order to answer the question: "What are the key limiting factors in this subject?" This search for the limiting factor occurs at a basic level when the problem is first identified, but now it is carried out at a deeper level. For example, a school is aware that students' reading comprehension is the key limiting factor to improving literacy results. However, the school now needs to define what specific reading comprehension skills are limiting factors to achieving the goal of improving reading comprehension. This can be done in several ways: zone analysis on a current data set, outcome analysis from students' current work samples, or a test that teachers create to check out a hunch about student needs or gaps.

Zone Analysis

A zone analysis focuses on the finer grain results in the area of the goal focus. For example, when looking to improve written language (the goal), one can usually turn to results from an assessment tool to see where the school's students fall short of the various standards it wants to meet.

Figure 6.2 provides data from the Australian NAPLAN (National Assessment Program—Literacy and Numeracy) assessment for one

	NAPLAN 2014												
						WRITING TASK							
Family Name	First Name	Audience /6	Text structure /4	Ideas /5	Persuasive devices /4	Vocabulary /5	Cohesion /4	Paragraphing /3	Sentence structure /6	Punctuation /5	Spelling /6	Total /48
					2		2		3			27
												37
			2		2		2					29
			2	2	2	2	2	1	2	2	2	20
			2						3			30
			2		2		2	1	3			26
			2		2	2	2		2	2	3	23
			2						3			30
			2		2	2	2		3			26
							2	1				32
							2		3			28
			2		2	2	2		3		3	26
							2		3			30
			2		2		2		3			27
			2		2		2		3			27
												37
									3			30
			2		2	2	2					28
							2					30
							2		3			32
			2		2	2	2		3	2		25
			2		2	2	2	1	3	2	3	23
			2		2			1				28
									3			34
			2		2	2	2					27

Figure 6.2. Zone Analysis on Written Language Standardised Assessment Results

class. The NAPLAN is an annual national assessment and, therefore, a source of lag data. In Figure 6.2, all the students' data from a written language test are set out by the specific learning outcomes tested and can easily be analysed to see where the school's weak points are. It may be an aspect such as the ability to produce ideas, the ability to use persuasive devices, the quality of sentence structure, or the use of paragraphs and punctuation. This school highlighted in red any test result where students scored 50% or fewer of the possible marks in the test. In that way, they could see the columns where red was predominant, indicating that most students had low achievement. In this class, sentence structure, cohesion, text structure, and use of persuasive devices are all heavily red. If this pattern were consistent across several classes, school leaders might initially focus on *improving sentence structure* as their first quick win, because that is a limiting factor for achieving the other areas of focus such as *improving paragraphs and punctuation*. However, all of these skills could be potential quick wins to be pursued by this school, though we recommend they do it by focusing on one—or at most two—at a time. Thus, the data could lead a school to decide on the following quick wins:

- QW1: Improve sentence structure;
- QW2: Improve paragraph structure;
- QW3: Improve punctuation;
- QW4: Improve use of persuasive devices.

In that way, a school could incrementally, but systematically, improve the quality of writing over a 4–6 month period, focusing on one quick win for about 4–6 weeks. Again, these quick wins are sought along-side business-as-usual. The purpose of writing is to communicate. The quick wins identified from these data are the technical skills underpinning the ability to communicate in writing. Teachers may be spending 15 minutes a day on the direct instruction of these and might have put in numerous strategies to enhance students' ability to monitor their own skill development by providing success criteria or using a peer feedback mechanism. The teacher would not de-emphasise the higher-level writing skills of conveying worthwhile information in a compelling way.

Outcome Analysis

If a school does not already have the finer-grained data represented in Figure 6.2, it can investigate student work samples to establish common errors across a group of students. For example, students' writing across the curriculum could be examined to determine trends. Common weaknesses could be identified and prioritised, starting with the most basic skills or the skills that are most likely to limit future progress.

Checking Hunches

Initial quick wins can also be established by reviewing sought outcomes from the syllabus and acting on hunches as to what may potentially be limiting factors. To do this, leaders must create a measurement tool so they can collect data on the outcomes that they suspect to be issues (see Chapter Seven), and then narrow it down to a few quick wins.

In one school where improving written language was identified as the priority goal—in particular, eliminating a weakness in punctuation and grammar—the SLT derived their quick win ideas from reviewing the syllabus outcomes. Once they identified the concepts that they believed to be most problematic, they tested those hunches with a group of students to see what was problematic when students wrote independently. From those data they determined their initial quick wins:

- QW1: Able to group related ideas into paragraphs;
- QW2: Able to select simple, compound, and complex sentences to connect ideas, occasionally manipulating the structure for emphasis, clarity, or effect;
- QW3: Able to use subordinating conjunctions—for example, "even though", as in "even though a storm was predicted, the search and enter mission still went ahead".

One teacher initially tested these hunches on her class. She had students write a piece of work and then marked them for their ability in the three quick wins. She knew that her students could group ideas into paragraphs, but her testing of these concepts showed her that the students did not do it when she was not prompting them. Changing that behaviour was established as a first quick win. The samples of work also indicated that the other two quick wins were gaps. Based on testing possible quick wins with a sample of students and developing a measurement tool, the quick win focus was established for several classes at that level of the school.

Are Quick Wins the Same Across the School?

Quick wins need to be the same across a group of teachers, but they are rarely the same across the whole school. There are several common approaches that appear to be effective.

The first is when the whole school has one goal, such as "Improve reading comprehension", but different parts of the school need to pursue quick wins that are relevant to their level or, in a secondary school, to their department. For example, in a primary school, the quick wins at Years 1 and 2 of a school would probably be different from those of Year 3 and 4 class levels, and so on. The following situation could be an example of how this would work.

Table 6.1. Example of Possible Quick Wins Across a Primary School

Goal: Improve Reading Comprehension	
Quick win for years 1 and 2	Improve student self-checking for sense as measured by self-correction rates.
Quick win for years 3 and 4	Improve students' ability to reflect on author voice as measured by pre- and post-cycle task.
Quick win for years 5 and 6	Improve students' ability to locate main point as measured by pre- and post-cycle task.

Another approach is to focus on one or two skills across the school as a quick win(s). This approach is common in primary schools but can also be used in secondary schools. One can focus on dispositions such as persistence in the face of challenge, or generic skills that enhance achievement in every learning area, such as improving reading or writing skills. An example of the latter is a secondary school that investigated issues with examination results and concluded that, while face value results were high, the school was not actually adding value to reading comprehension levels. In fact, they had negative growth or regression of results when the data were analysed by an external expert. Therefore, they decided to trial an approach to improving comprehension skills across the whole cohort. They started by conducting zone analysis on their literacy results, and from their findings they were able to narrow down some key areas of concern. These areas of concern were the ability of students to locate a main idea, make an inference, and understand vocabulary.

The school decided to focus on the quick win of locating a main idea, because the higher-level skill of inferencing requires the ability to locate a main idea and to know the meaning of vocabulary. Vocabulary development requires a long-term strategy, but teaching students to locate a main idea could be enabled by teaching a strategy in a relatively short time frame. Thus, *locating a main idea in a text* became their first quick win across the whole school.

Equally, though, in a secondary school, the tasks associated with quick wins might differ from department to department in pursuit of a goal—for example, for every student *passing the course* or attaining a certain level of expertise. O'Keeffe College, the school featured in Chapter Three, developed an approach of asking each department to name two or three key milestones for each course they taught each term. These key milestones, their quick wins, had to be critical "must learns" or "must dos" for their courses. These were entered into an electronic mark-book where, at the end of the term, a teacher marked each student as having achieved the milestone or not: a simple Yes/ No decision. At the end of the term, the students and their parents received a printout of the students' milestones from each course. The printout looked something like Table 6.2.

Table 6.2. Example of Milestone or Quick Win Report in a Secondary School

Subject	Milestone	Achieved (Yes/No)
English—Term One	Complete a reading log of at least 3 books including one biography.	Y
Science—Term One	Write an 800-word essay explaining photosynthesis.	Y
Physical Education— Term One	Demonstrate correct softball throw.	Y
	Teach a group of younger students the throw.	N

In this way, the senior leadership devolved the creation of quick wins to heads of department and individual teachers who oversaw courses. It forced teachers to be clear about what was important. It would be possible for a secondary school to have a mix of a whole-school and a departmentalised approach by having, for example, two cycles of 5 weeks on a common goal such as a literacy-related quick win.

Then, for the remainder of the year, a school could pursue the milestone approach, as O'Keeffe College did. This mixed approach could be particularly powerful in the junior years of secondary school. At senior levels, where examination requirements tend to be constraints, a departmentalised approach would probably be most effective.

The senior leadership team's role is to ensure there is a coherent approach to achieving a school's goal through quick wins. Their job is to monitor the quality and nature of the quick wins, and to put in place the timelines and systems to ensure that quick wins are pursued.

Key Points

Good quick wins:

- are usually attained using a *common needs* or a *target student* approach;
- are a valuable outcome in their own right;
- address a limiting factor that impacts a signficant number of students;
- are a reliable predictor of the longer-term goal;
- are something that is readily embedded in the day-to-day work;
- are easily measured;
- are achieved in short timeframes, often ranging from around 3 to 6 weeks in primary schools and no more than 10 weeks in secondary schools;
- energise and excite staff and students to keep trying different things to get different results;
- accumulate, moving a school closer to realising its longer-term strategic and annual student-centred goals.

References

Amabile, T., & Kramer, S. J. (2011). The power of small wins. *Harvard Business Review*, *89*(5), 1–12.

Bandura, A. (1993). Perceived self-efficacy in cognitive development and functioning. *Educational Psychologist, 28*(2), 117–148.

Bryk, A. S., Gomez, L. M., Grunow, A., & LeMahieu, P. G. (2015). *Learning to improve: How America's schools can get better at getting better.* Harvard Education Press.

Donohoo, J. (2017). *Collective efficacy: How educators' beliefs impact student learning.* Corwin.

Hattie, J. (2015). *The politics of collaborative expertise.* Pearson.

Klein, H. J., Wesson, M. J., Hollenbeck, J. R., & Alge, B. J. (1999). Goal commitment and the goal-setting process: Conceptual clarification and empirical synthesis. *Journal of Applied Psychology, 84*(6), 885–896.

Meyers, C. V., & Hitt, D. H. (2018). Planning for school turnaround in the United States: An analysis of the quality of principal-developed quick wins. *School Effectiveness and School Improvement, 29*(3), 362–382.

Timperley, H., Kaser, L., & Halbert, J. (2014). *A framework for transforming learning in schools: Innovation and the spiral of inquiry.* Centre for Strategic Education.

Weick, K. E. (1984). Small wins: Redefining the scale of social problems. *American Psychological Association, 39*(1), 40–49.

CHAPTER SEVEN

Developing the Measures and Establishing the Baseline

The next steps in developing a theory of improvement are developing and testing quick-win measures and identifying the baseline. In this chapter, we outline the two major types of measures required: student outcome and process measures. Further, we discuss the need to test the measures and how to establish a baseline as part of this process. This testing step allows refinement of the quick win, the measure, and the short-term pedagogical strategy before implementing improvement strategies. Finally, we discuss how graphs can be used to present and examine data.

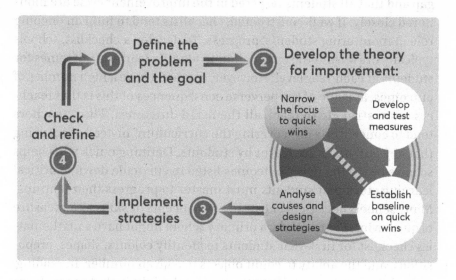

Figure 7.1. The School Improvement Cycle: Develop and Test Measures, and Establish a Baseline

A minimum of two kinds of measures are required to understand and respond to the impact of improvement cycles: student outcome measures and process measures. Student outcome measures are measures of students' ability to master quick wins. Process measures are indicators of how effective the school and teachers are in implementing the improvement strategies. Other aspects that schools might want to measure are students' or teachers' attitudes, dispositions, and competencies. We describe these measures, along with examples of how to develop them.

Student Outcome Measures

Typical quick-win measures used for students include checklists, rubrics, observations, surveys, or self-/peer assessments.

Checklists

Checklists are vital for ensuring that students do not slip through a gap and that all students targeted in the improvement cycle are monitored closely. If well-constructed, checklists tend to fulfil an ongoing role in monitoring students' progress. To develop a checklist, schools typically draw from the curriculum to identify learning outcomes for students at each year level. However, curricula have a high number of outcomes, and one of the perverse consequences of this is that teachers often struggle to teach all the listed outcomes. Thus, teachers tend to concentrate on "covering the curriculum" instead of ensuring that key outcomes are learnt by students. Defining quick wins helps schools refine the many outcomes listed in curricula down to critical learning steps that students must master to progress their learning. Many schools devise checklists of key concepts or skills as a measure of quick wins. For example, a primary school might have a mathematics checklist for first-year students to identify colours, shapes, prepositions, and the ability to count objects to a given number. In reading, a checklist for the first 6 months at school might include some basic sight words, alphabet names, and sound knowledge.

When all teachers agree on what the "essentials" are at a given year level, and checklists are used and acted upon regularly, checklists ensure that agreed priorities are not forgotten. The data from these checklists can identify the common "sticking points" that many students are experiencing, and a team of teachers can pursue strategies to address these collaboratively.

When using a checklist, one rule of thumb is that the mastery of a skill should not be "ticked off" until it has been witnessed multiple times in different contexts over some time. Demonstrating a competency once does not mean it is mastered. This point is made in the left-hand column of the mathematics checklist provided as an example in Figure 7.2. The example shows a common approach to a checklist where all students are recorded in the left-hand column and dates are inserted in the appropriate column when the behaviour has been observed at least three times and the teacher and student are confident that the skill or concept is mastered. The format ensures that students' needs can be readily identified across the group of students (quick wins) and remedied with instruction.

Jan 2021		GP1		GP2			
		Beginning Year 1		End Year 1 / Beginning Year 2			End Year 2
		MAe-6NA / MA1-6NA		MA1-6NA			
		Count by ones to find a total of a group	Shares collections equally 1 to 1	Solve multiplication problems by grouping objects	Solve division problems by sharing in groups (not 1 by 1)	Skip count by 2's, 5's and tens to find to total number of objects	Solve times as many multiplication problems with partial models
Growth Point Descriptions. To be observed at least three times							

Figure 7.2. Example of a Checklist

When teachers consistently use a checklist across a group of students, it ensures that all teachers teach and monitor agreed priorities. Over time, this becomes business-as-usual and helps ensure high standards. As the saying goes, "What gets measured, gets done". As a result of using checklists, a teacher can readily identify specific individual goals for target students, or the teacher can form groups of students to teach to common needs. Checklists help safeguard against students falling through gaps in the system and guide teachers on what outcomes to focus on.

Rubrics

Rubrics are commonly used tools in school improvement efforts to enhance the school's ability to ensure that the changes they make truly result in improvement. Rubrics measure changes in student learning outcomes by capturing a description of varying standards of performance. While checklists record a behaviour mastered or achieved, rubrics provide finer-grained results. Rubrics can provide information about the next steps to improvement or an indication of the frequency of a student behaviour, because when a behaviour is consistently observed, it is an indication of mastery.

Criterion-referenced rubrics provide descriptive details of the development of students' knowledge and thus steps for improvement. They are more frequently used in secondary schools where more fine-grained performance indicators are required. The example depicted in Figure 7.3 is meant to be read from the bottom of each column, where quick-win outcomes are stated. As the reader moves up a column, they view more advanced indicators of the outcome. The school may focus on one outcome at a time or all three at once, as the concepts overlap somewhat. The baseline data from such a rubric will demonstrate the areas of greatest need.

The next two examples show how a primary school initially designed a criterion-referenced rubric derived from the curriculum (see Figure 7.4) that they later adapted to a frequency rubric (see Figure 7.5), which they found easier to use. The criterion-referenced rubric is designed to be read across the rows from left to right, with each row indicating a different quick win. It spells out the criteria for levels of achievement in aspects of written language that had been identified as problematic from a national assessment.

After some trialling, teachers at the school moved to a frequency rubric that they found easier to use. In this rubric (see Figure 7.5), there is only one key skill per row, and teachers mark the frequency with which students display this behaviour from *not evident* to *consistently evident*.

Criterion Referenced Rubric

1.3 Varies the use of inclusive language and personal pronouns to make an authorial connection with the reader	2.3 Uses a variety of techniques such as a hook, anecdote or rhetorical question to 'draw' the reader in	3.3 Connects with the reader by developing a shared understanding of the context with a range of persuasive techniques	4.3 Language choice appeals to the emotions of the reader and is precise, effective and sophisticated
1.2 Establishes strong, credible voice that helps associate the author and the reader.	2.2 Uses some techniques such as imagery, examples etc., to engage the reader's interest.	3.2 Connects with the reader by developing a common ground with some persuasive techniques.	4.2 Language choice has emotional elements that help connect the reader
1.1 Develops some relationship with reader (e.g., polite, formal, social distance, personal connection)	2.1 Presents a position with an idea outlined	3.1 Demonstrates a basic awareness of audience by attempting to orient the reader	4.1 Simple words used to make some connection with the reader
Insufficient evidence	Insufficient evidence	Insufficient evidence	Insufficient evidence
1. Connects with reader through authorial voice	**2. Engages reader (interest)**	**3. Connects with reader for shared understanding**	**4. Emotional connection with reader**
Demonstrates awareness of the intended audience by attempting to orient the reader			

Figure 7.3. Example of a Criterion-referenced Rubric from a Secondary School

Year 3 Rubric	0	1 CrT6	2 CrT7	3 CrT8
Sentence structure	Not evident	Writes simple sentences correctly *including some correct simple punctuation*	Writes simple sentences correctly *including correct simple punctuation*	Writes simple sentences correctly *consistently using correct punctuation*
Sentence Use	Not evident	Writes simple and compound sentences related to a topic using conjunctions (and, but, so, because, when)	Writes compound sentences to make connections between ideas using coordinating conjunctions (and, but, so)	Writes complex sentences using conjunctions (when, because)
Text Organisation	Not evident	Organises text logically (ideas in time sequence)	Organises text and supports ideas with some detail and elaboration	Organises ideas to support the reader (uses chronological sequencing)
Text Cohesion	Not evident	Uses pronouns correctly to link to an object or person	Consistently uses pronouns correctly to link to an object or person across the text	Uses pronouns to track multiple characters (Peter and Leanne … he … they … she … them)
Tense	Not evident	Maintains tense within a sentence	Maintains consistent tense within and between sentences	Tense mostly correct throughout text

Figure 7.4. Example of a Criterion-referenced Rubric from a Primary School

Descriptors for rubrics measuring frequency usually range from *not evident* to *sometimes evident,* to *usually evident,* and finally to *consistently evident.* However, other frequency steps can be used. Frequency rubrics are positively loaded, meaning they go from a behaviour *not being evident* to *being evident to different degrees,* with most descriptors referring to how, or how often, the behaviour is evident. Criterion-referenced rubrics present different levels of mastery

Stage 2 Rubric		Not evident 0	Sometimes 1	Usually 2	Consistently 3
Sentence use and structure	Writes sentences correctly including correct simple punctuation				
	Writes a variety of sentences using simple, compound and complex				
Text Organisation	Organises text and supports ideas with detail and elaboration				
Cohesion (tense)	Maintains tense within and between sentences				

Figure 7.5. Example of a Frequency Rubric from a Primary School

of a skill. It can be challenging to construct criteria for each step in the progression. The steps need to be clearly delineated from one descriptor to the next so that it is clear when the next step is reached. Further, the rubric should show an even amount of progress between steps, which means advancing from step one to two should relate to equal progress from step two to step three. The following three rules of thumb can help develop and use a rubric.

First, there should be only one skill to judge in each column or row. If multiple skills are measured in one column or row, it is difficult to score and reduces reliability, as a student may have mastered one, but not the other, skill. Teachers need to be able to make a definitive judgment about which score the student is assigned.

Second, a consistent practice for teachers should be to assign the lower grade if in doubt about where the student sits on the rubric. For example, if teachers are unsure if the student fits into the *usually* or the *sometimes* category, they should record *sometimes*. This rule of thumb ensures that all teachers are conservative in their judgments, thereby creating a higher degree of reliability. Furthermore, there is a *ceiling effect* in any tool. Students who have mastered the skill and reached the "top" of the rubric cannot show further progress. The fewer students at the ceiling of the rubric, the more useful the tool is to both the teacher and the student. Marking downwards minimises the ceiling effect.

Third, if the rubric is a four-step rubric, the third step should be aligned to the age-appropriate achievement of the skill that all students should achieve. For example, in a frequency rubric, this would be a behaviour being *usually evident.* Not many people are faultless all the time. Thus, mastery of a specific skill needs to be evident most, but not all, of the time. The fourth step should describe achievement above where most students might be expected to perform. Again, this avoids a ceiling effect and leaves room to record students who achieve higher. Other examples of descriptors that have been used by schools we have worked with are:

needs lots of help—on the way—got it;
unacceptable—needs work—competent—sophisticated;
poor—satisfactory—good—excellent;
not evident—developing—competent—exemplary;
not evident—developing—basic—competent—advanced.

Tests

Other ways to establish a baseline are tests checking key concepts or skills. Tests provide information to teachers about who in the class has the requisite knowledge or skills and who does not. The quick win focuses on explicit teaching for the students with a common gap in a specific skill. The follow-up test, at the check and refine step, is usually a similar test with a different set of items.

For example, in the excerpt of the test depicted in Figure 7.6, the teacher created items to check all key concepts within one domain of mathematics (place value) that the teacher had concerns about. When the items were marked, the teacher identified the common problems to focus on as the first quick wins. After a period of direct instruction on these problems over about a month, the teacher re-tested the students on a parallel version of the test, i.e., a similar test but with different numbers in the test items. The improvement was significant and quick because the teacher could precisely target the sticking points for students. The teacher commented that, while we talk about making learning visible, what he and his colleagues found from developing this test and gathering data was that neither the students nor their teachers were aware of the specific needs of each student and the common needs across the class until they carried out this exercise.

Given the approach's success, it was shared with other teachers and scaled up. The initial trial and the sharing of the success of the deliberate acts of teaching that followed the identification of gaps in student knowledge led to other teachers adopting the same approach by creating similar tests suitable for their year levels.

```
9.   Your teacher will call out some numbers and you are to write them down below.

     a)            b)            c)            d)            e)

     f)                          g)                          h)

10.   Put the following sets of numbers from smallest to largest.

Set A:  8   3   2   _____

Set B: 23  49  21  _____

Set C: 936  45  478  _____

Set D:       8392   4539   9263

     _____


11.   What is this number?              Answer: _____
      How do you know?                  Answer: _____
```

Figure 7.6. Excerpt from a Pencil and Paper Test on Place Value Concepts

Tests can focus on any set of outcomes. The example in Figure 7.7 comes from a school seeking information on students' ability to make an inference from a written text. The test is a simple short story with inference questions. Teachers marked whether students could extract information from the text to make correct inferences. As a follow-up test, the school used a different short story with similar questions. A test might be used alongside a rubric noting students' ability to locate relevant information and apply it to make an inference in relation to specific criteria or frequency.

Observations

Another measure to check progress and record quick wins is observation. For example, a teacher can observe a group of students carrying

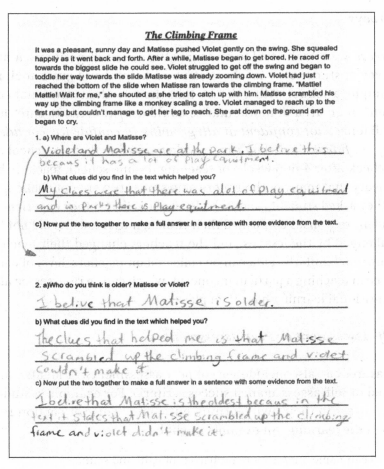

Figure 7.7. Paper and Pencil Inference Test

out a problem-solving exercise and note who uses appropriate processes and who does not. Or a teacher checks which students in each reading group can summarise the main idea, recording their observations with a simple Yes/No judgment. This task could be carried out over 2 weeks to get a picture of every student's ability. The students with a common gap in their skills could be targeted for that quick-win instruction. The information gleaned from observations is usually recorded on rubrics or checklists. Using a rubric or checklist or a similar form of observation guide ensures that the focus of the observation is clear.

Surveys

Surveys are a useful tool to measure attitudes or dispositions. A brief survey of students or teachers can be a helpful and quick tool. For example, a school with a theory that their students were not confident in an area of mathematics could ask students to rate their confidence: *not confident at all*; *growing in confidence*; *confident*; *very confident*. Such data can provide a baseline that the school can re-check after 4 or 5 weeks of teaching. In one school, teachers had a theory that many of their more able students were not challenged, so they asked students about the level of challenge they experienced. Student responses confirmed their hunch; most students did not feel challenged by the lessons, and the teachers changed their teaching approach. Similarly, data can be collected on teachers' level of confidence in teaching a particular concept, which can be re-assessed after professional learning has taken place.

Self-Assessment or Peer Assessment

Measures can also include self- or peer assessments. Students can be asked to self-assess against success criteria. For example, a student may attest to their own learning outcomes. This very action reinforces the learning. An example might be:

> "I can name one/or more properties of light and sound;
>
> I can explain how light/sound is transformed into other types of energy;
>
> I can discuss how light/sound enable us to communicate."
>
> (Excerpt from Table 4.2, Hattie, 2012, p. 62)

An assessment can be made through a class discussion about the properties of light and sound at the beginning of a science unit. Students can rate their own knowledge against specific criteria. If the class had not come across the concepts before, teachers might expect a generally low level of knowledge, which could be confirmed or disconfirmed. At the end of the unit, the students could again self- or peer-assess their knowledge. The teacher could spot check those data by observing the pairs of students interacting. Thus, pre- and post-teaching assessments do not have to be teacher-driven. Students can take ownership and enhance their learning by doing so.

Attitudes, Disposition, and Competency Measures

The measures described above can also be used to measure attitudes, dispositions, or competencies of students and teachers. For example, schools often want to improve students' self-management, but that concept is too broad to measure without being refined to explicit examples of self-management. To develop a rubric for self-management, staff need to reflect on what they are seeing that leads them to be concerned about self-management and identify specific behaviours that are evident when students do manage their own learning and select one behaviour to focus on at a time. Table 7.1 presents some behaviours observed by teachers and behaviours they identified that can indicate self-management.

Table 7.1. Highlighting Indicators of Competencies—Student Self-management

Self-management— what we are seeing	Self-management— what we want to see
• frequently come to class without the right gear	• bring necessary equipment to class, e.g., pens; tablets/computers; physical education gear
• frequently fail to complete and hand in homework	• complete and hand in homework
• frequently late	• get to class on time

Having discussed the observed behaviours versus desired behaviours, teachers might focus on one or two of those behaviours and develop a rubric to measure quick wins and establish a baseline. The example below shows how "getting to class on time" could be measured.

Table 7.2. Example Rubric for "Getting to Class on Time"

Being punctual to class	Almost never (1–2 times a month)	Sometimes (1–2 times a week)	Usually (0–1 time late per month)	Consistently (always punctual)

In this instance, it would be useful for teachers to gather data over a month to establish a baseline, i.e., to assess where students sit on the rubric. Once the baseline is identified, an agreed strategy to encourage punctuality could be implemented for a month while teachers record data on how often students are late to class. These data could be compared to the baseline, and improvement ideas refined in response. These measures can also be used to gather data from teachers. For example, if part of the theory was that teachers lacked confidence in their ability to teach a subject area, this idea would have to be tested using a measure of teacher confidence. After strategies to address this concern had been implemented, teachers' confidence would be measured again to ascertain change.

Process Measures

Besides the data on student outcomes, data are also required on the processes and strategies used to get quick-wins results. For example, if the quick win was related to improving students' knowledge of the properties of light and sound, the leadership team would need to establish systems so they understood what teachers were doing to achieve that outcome. If strategies were agreed on, they would need to know whether teachers actually enacted them. If the strategies were not enacted and highly variable results from class to class were evident after the *implement strategies* step, a school would not know why they got the results they did. Was it due to ineffective strategy, or was it due to ineffective implementation by teachers? There are easy ways to establish whether teachers implemented agreed-upon teaching strategies. It is important that these measures are transparent to teachers, so everyone knows what to expect and understands and agrees with the data-collection methods.

Schools can use three common process measures: teacher reporting on actions and impact, observations by an expert or staff member, and student reports. First, schools can establish a system whereby teachers report back mid-cycle or after a few weeks on their actions and early indications of impact. It should be clear what and how teachers are reporting back. For example, a leadership team may produce a template that illustrates what teachers should report back on. This might include how often the concept was revisited in teaching, what activities were used, the teachers' sense of its success and shortcomings to date, and any challenges and recommendations. A template or guide for reporting ensures that reports by teachers cover the same topics and foci. This also enables aggregating the data for an across-school overview.

Second, an external or internal expert can make observations across classrooms and report back to groups of teachers on trends observed and recommendations for further actions. Observation and feedback can be helpful to support teachers in their implementation early or midway in the cycle. This approach was taken in Gauguin Primary, the case study school described in Chapter Two. Here, deputy principals observed teachers in their pod groups and provided feedback to the group as a basis for discussions on the next steps.

A third process measure involves asking students to report back on what they have experienced in the teaching of quick-win skills. Schools can collect data with a brief survey involving one or two questions or interviewing a sample of students from each class. One school videoed some of the students providing feedback about the changes in pedagogical practice—what they had noticed and how they had reacted to the changes. They shared the videos in a staff meeting. It was an eye-opener for staff and a great motivator for changing practice.

In particular, we have found the first process measure simple to use and very effective. Asking teachers to report back is unobtrusive and shows trust in teachers to be doing what was agreed to. However, it also creates a certain level of accountability for teachers because they have to stand in front of their peers to report on their actions and progress. Sharing what has worked—and what has not—enables learning for the whole team or school.

Important Steps when Creating Measures

Designing a measure can be quite challenging. Three important steps are highlighted in the following paragraphs. A key role for school leaders is ensuring that any measures are carefully developed and that staff have guidelines on how to use them.

Creating Agreement on Terms and Descriptors

It is crucial that there is discussion and agreement about what the terms and descriptors used in the measure mean (e.g., sometimes, usually, or consistently). Does *sometimes* mean two or three times a week? Does *usually* mean most of the time? And does *consistently* mean almost unfailingly? Numbers need to be put on these terms (e.g., sometimes = 2x per week) so that measurement is reliable across teaching teams.

Maximising Reliability

Reliability means that no matter who scored the student's work, they come up with the same judgment on the student's level of achievement on the measure. Reliability can only be assured by clear definitions, agreement on the terms used, and moderation. Moderation involves a teacher making a judgment about the level of achievement of a piece of work and comparing it to the original judgment by another teacher, with any differences being discussed. The process of moderating helps to ensure that the data are reliable and helps teachers learn from each other about what standard they expect of students.

Ensuring Validity

The first round of data collection is a test of the measure's usefulness. We advise initially checking the measure with just a few students to see if it produces the kind of information sought and whether the initial data collection validates the quick win as a real gap in students' learning. This is a check on its validity: "Does it measure what we want to measure? Is it showing a gap in student learning, or have they already mastered this?" The following section describes this step in more detail.

Testing Measures and Establishing the Baseline

Once a quick win measure has been developed, it needs to be tested with a few students or one class to establish whether it does what it sets out to do and whether the quick wins are, in fact, the learning gap that was hypothesised. The data from that small test of the measure needs to be graphed so that teachers can answer the question: "Is there really a problem to solve here?" This provides the basis for the school to either refine the tool or refine the areas that need to be checked to see if they are indeed appropriate quick wins. This short, initial testing of the measure and the appropriateness of the quick wins has several advantages. First, one enthusiastic teacher can do the testing, so others do not have to use their time at this stage. If the tool or the quick wins do not turn out to be appropriate, most teachers have not experienced any frustration associated with that. A teacher who is an early adopter of this process is more likely to want to refine the tool and trial it again. Second, when the teacher who does the testing reports back to other teachers with a graph of the results and feedback on the measurement tool, it usually motivates other teachers. They want to see the results for their students. Finally, the early-adopter teacher often becomes a *teacher-leader* of colleagues; their testing of the process often leads to this process being seen as driven from the middle of the school.

Thus, this *testing* step is very different from the *implement strategies* step. It allows the big theoretical idea about how achieving a quick win will move the school towards its goal to be tested before presenting the idea to the wider staff. Some schools take this stage further and test the initial pedagogical strategy that they are advocating to address the quick win before presenting the "story" to the wider staff. The heads of department in one secondary school, for example, developed tools and strategies and tested them with their own classes and graphed their results before collectively presenting the strategies and results to the wider staff. In this case, the leadership team's testing of their theory and their willingness to put the hard work into developing tools and strategies that were well-researched to address the student needs showed staff that leaders were "walking their talk". They were not asking teachers to do anything that they had not already tested and seen as effective, and they had the evidence to show it. Having tested the approach, they really understood it, were powerful advocates for the approach, and were in a position to lead their teams in the implementation.

We next present a few examples of how measures can be tested and what schools can learn from those tests. As the baseline data in Figure 7.8 illustrate, one teacher first sought data on three writing outcomes with a rubric on whether students could use the concepts consistently. The first outcome was to *group ideas into paragraphs*. The first group of bars in the graph show that most students did not use paragraphs. The teacher was horrified, as she had expected students to be able to do this. "How did I not know this?" she questioned on gathering these data. For the assessment, the students wrote in front of the teacher without support from her or fellow students. The teacher's theory on students' apparent lack of the skill was that when the students were writing in the classroom, she would wander around and prompt them to use paragraphs. However, the data showed that the students were not using the skill independently. The independent use of the skill thus became her first quick win to work on. The second group of bars in the graph refers to an outcome related to selecting simple compound and complex sentences to enhance writing. The third group of bars is using subordinating conjunctions, for example, using "even though". The teacher felt that the first skill was the most important to develop. Using subordinating conjunctions was the second quick win, as the evidence suggested few were using them. Thus, this test of her rubric established that the rubric was measuring what it was meant to measure, and it helped her determine what the priority quick wins were to work on. It also provided her with a baseline.

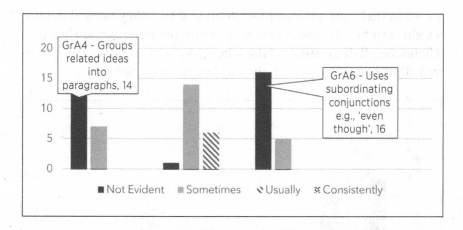

Figure 7.8. Year 6 Writing Assessment

Figure 7.9 describes another example where one teacher initially tested the measure with just five students. The school's theory was that students often recognised spelling or punctuation errors but did not necessarily address them. Therefore, they established a process of a "quick write" where students wrote briefly, had editing time, and had the opportunity to demonstrate their grasp on the school's approach to recrafting, which involved using editing keys (standard processes for showing that a student recognises a spelling or punctuation error, such as circling a spelling error). The school's theory was that many students recognised errors, but they did not go back and try to correct them. The first trial with just five students, while not representative of the whole school, allowed them to test their processes and their approach to measuring them, and to share the results with staff. Following that small test of the process, they moved to a larger test across several classes. They found that many students had few errors, so they did not have evidence of their efforts to correct those errors. The question arose: "Were the students playing it safe and not using vocabulary that they could not spell or punctuation that they were uncertain of?" This led to another amendment in the measure: teachers were asked to annotate the students' data with a comment about the degree of vocabularly and punctuation use and not just concentrate on their corrections. They also found that teachers varied in their instructions to students and that they needed to have a tight script for teachers to use to ensure the process was rigorous. Therefore, all this testing set the school up not to waste teachers' time and effort once they were in the *implement strategies* step.

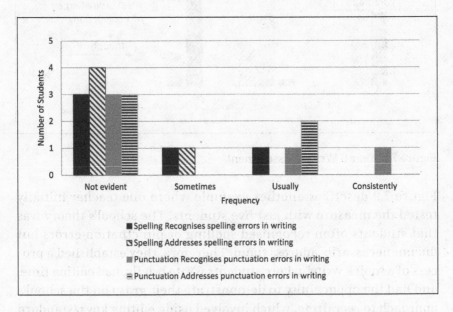

Figure 7.9. Baseline Data From One Class to Test Quick Wins and the Measurement Tool of Students' Editing Strategies

Using Graphs to Present and Examine Data

Once the baseline data on the potential quick wins are gathered, it is important to collate and graph the data. Bar graphs, in particular, make the visual presentation of the degree of improvement over the course of the cycle more powerful than a table of data. Table 7.3 displays how schools set out their data, which facilitates graphing it, as in Figure 7.10.

Presenting data in this manner allows a team of teachers to see that they have made some positive shifts from their baseline (Time 1 data in Table 7.3 and Figure 7.10) in impacting the level of challenge in their lessons, but there is still a lot of room for improvement. Talking to students about why they answered the way they did would

Table 7.3. Pre- and Post-Action Data on "Is the Work You Are Doing in Class Challenging?"

Student response	Time 1	Time 2
Yes	16%	26%
No	28%	24%
Sometimes	56%	50%

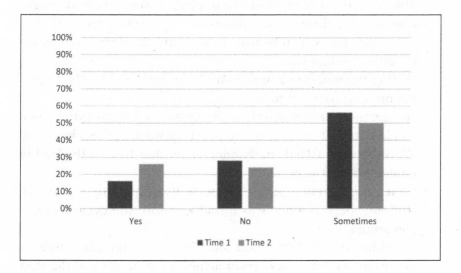

Figure 7.10. Bar Graph Presentation of Pre- and Post-Action Data on "Is the Work You Are Doing in Class Challenging?"

help teachers flesh out their theory for improvement and inform their next steps to improve results in the next cycle. This is why we are explicit, in our School Improvement Cycle, that this measuring step can lead back to more theorising about causes and revisiting thinking about the optimal quick wins or pedagogical approach. For example, if the inquiry with students revealed that many students would be more challenged if they had a greater choice in the tasks they could complete, that finding could lead to a different strategy for teachers to employ in the *implement strategy* step of the next cycle—such as teachers providing two or three options with varying levels of challenge in a task. Or adding an "Extra for Experts" challenge on top of the standard task for all students so that those who feel they can go further with their learning have the opportunity to do so.

Key Points

- There are at least two types of measures required for each cycle: an *outcome measure* focused on quick wins for students, and a *process measure* focused on the implementation of the strategy.
- Checklists, rubrics, tests, observations, surveys, and self- and peer assessments can be used to measure the degree of change in student outcomes.
- Testing the measure is important to ensure validity: "Is it measuring what we want to measure?"
- Testing the measure and the strategy with a few students by one teacher initially prevents timewasting for most teachers and allows an enthusiastic early-adopter teacher to take the lead in implementing the cycle.
- Collecting baseline data is important to knowing where the students' performance was initially, before the cycle was implemented.
- Graphing the baseline data and the data after each cycle is important as it makes current achievement levels and the shift in results more obvious and motivating than a table of data. Bar graphs are recommended for clarity in comparing pre- and post-data.

References

Hattie, J. (2012). *Visible learning for teachers: Maximising impact on learning*. Routledge.

CHAPTER EIGHT

Analysing Causes and Designing Strategies

This chapter outlines how the overarching theory for improvement is formally developed. Theory development entails a few key steps: analysing the root causes of the problem, which is usually referred to as *causal analysis*; checking the validity of one's thinking about causes; theorising or hypothesising about the appropriate strategies to respond to those causes; and checking the validity of the hypotheses. Without this formal analysis, a school is at risk of simply pursuing random quick wins, or worse, thinking that the cause of the problem lies only in the quality of the teaching.

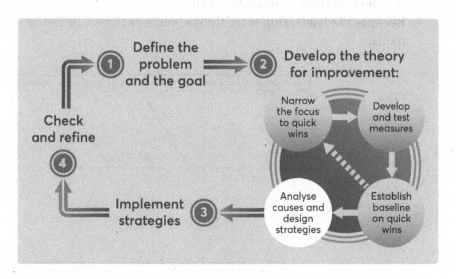

Figure 8.1. The School Improvement Cycle: Analyse Causes and Design Strategies

Causal Analysis—The Fishbone and Five Whys

The first step in developing a theory for improvement is to undertake a causal analysis to better understand the nature of the problem and what may be causing it. One effective method of carrying out structured brainstorming about causes of the problem is to use a fishbone diagram and follow that process through using up to five *whys*. The fishbone is a diagram that has the problem clearly defined at the head of the *fish*, and then each major bone off the spine of the fish is used to define a possible major cause of this problem. The *five whys* constitute a process where the facilitator of the development of the fishbone diagram asks, "Why is that happening?". They might ask that up to five times, depending on the answers, with the aim of getting to the root cause of the problem.

For example:

1. Teachers may not spend adequate time teaching reading—Why?
2. Because there are a lot of subjects to teach in a primary school—Why is that problematic?
3. Because no minimum times have been put in place to guide teachers on subject priorities—Why?
4. Because the leadership team thinks teachers should be autonomous.

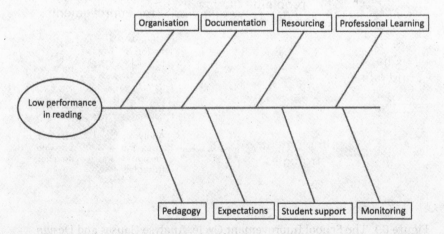

Figure 8.2. The Fishbone for Low Performance in Reading with Pre-Populated Headings

To facilitate this process, the leader draws up the head of the fish and puts the clearly articulated *problem* in it. The problem should be student-centred and based on data, as discussed in the previous chapter on defining the problem. In Figure 8.2, the problem is defined as "*Low performance in reading*", meaning that schools serving a similar population are performing a lot better. Next, each major bone represents a key cause thought to contribute to this problem. To get teachers to think more diversely about causes of problems, it can be helpful to pre-populate the major bones with broad potential educational causes such as leadership; teaching methods; resources; systems; student support; professional knowledge; and expectations, as we have in Figure 8.2. Next, we outline a hypothetical case of developing a fishbone.

In our hypothetical case, teachers firstly theorised that students do not get a lot of exposure to books at home. Teachers often focus on student- or family-centred problems first—such as "not having books at home". These should only be captured in the diagram if the school is realistically able to influence those factors. In this example, when asked "why" students do not have books at home, the teachers pointed to the school's policies. The school had a policy that if a student lost a book, they could not take another book home until the lost book was found and returned. When asked why, it was a purely economic response about the cost of replacing books, and staff concluded that having an adequate annual book-replacement budget would be a better response if the school wanted to encourage reading at home. Thus, the discussion about the problem cause started from "a lack of support for students at home" but ended up being a school resourcing issue, as illustrated in Figure 8.3.

Ultimately, costs are a constraint on solving any problem. The school has to decide where its dollars are best spent when seeking a solution. If lack of home reading is a significant cause of the problem, and therefore the promotion of reading at home is seen as a valid part of the solution, that implies that more money should be allocated to it. The real reason for this problem, therefore, may be that inadequate resources are allocated to reading when it is supposed to be a priority. In that way, in three "whys", the school team found one possible source of the problem. The source is usually organisational in one form or another.

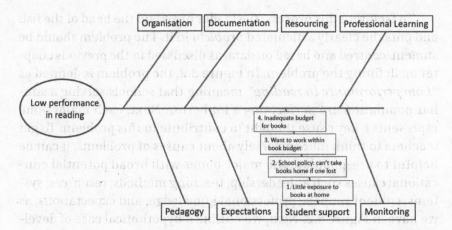

Figure 8.3. Applying "Why" to the Potential Cause of Little Exposure to Books at Home

A key question the facilitator of the process should ask is: "Can we impact that?" It is important for the person facilitating this brainstorming stage of the process to not let the brainstorming go into a blame mode where the causes of the problem are located in everyone else except the people doing the theorising, i.e., the teachers and leaders. However, some student-centred causes may be quite valid and can be acted upon, such as students not completing homework, which could be due to organisational factors such as inconsistent practices, poorly designed homework, or poor communication between home and school.

But there are some factors impacting learning that are out of the school's realm of influence—for example, poverty. While these wider social issues can be acknowledged as having an impact, they should not be included in the fishbone diagram. The leader's role when facilitating this process is to find the educational causes, particularly those that originate within the school.

The major causal factors should centre on what the process of (in this case) teaching reading involves in the school: how it is organised, led, and resourced. In Figure 8.4, the teachers next hypothesised that teacher expectations could be an influencing factor. For example, one teacher may think that expectations vary because the school does not set benchmarks for student progress. Therefore, teachers have different expectations of when students should move up a book level. When asked "why", it may be because leaders value teachers' independence and professionalism, and therefore they do not impose any set standards. Why will they not impose any set standards? Leaders often do not want to appear as not trusting teachers. Or perhaps they fear that teachers will oppose standards. Through the discussion and mapping answers to "why" on the fishbone diagram, leaders and teachers have the opportunity to discuss their values and beliefs openly. The value placed on teacher independence needs to be weighed up against what benefits students. Total teacher independence is likely in conflict with having high expectations for all students. The guiding principle should be: What is best for students? A school can have both a degree of teacher autonomy and also agreed bottom lines and systems that optimise outcomes for students.

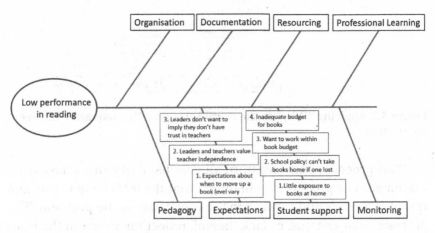

Figure 8.4. Applying Three "Whys" to the Possible Cause of Varying Teacher Expectations

Similarly, the school's guidelines for time spent on reading may be deemed problematic (see Figure 8.5). When asked "why" the time spent on teaching reading may not be adequate, teachers note the pressure of teaching several subjects and the limited time available. When asked "why" there is limited time, it seems that no minimum time has been set by the leadership team to guide teachers in how to balance the pressures of various curricula. When asked "why" the teachers are feeling this pressure, the response might be that leaders are not taking responsibility for helping teachers prioritise. It is left to individual teachers to allocate time to different subjects. The discussion could then revolve around how much time is required to teach all students adequately in reading over the course of a week versus other subjects. This theorising is captured in the fishbone diagram as illustrated in Figure 8.5.

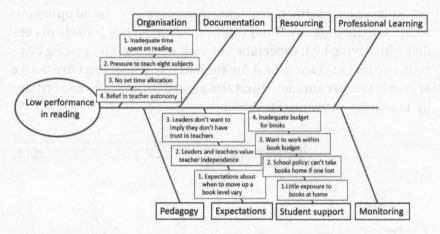

Figure 8.5. Applying "Why" to the Possible Cause of Inadequate Time Spent on Reading

This process continues until all possible root causes have been examined. The process may highlight that the leadership team's and teachers' beliefs and values are the root cause of the problem. The processes and systems, or lack thereof, reflect the values of the leaders. The fishbone and the five-why process help to move the discussion from the surface-level symptoms to these root causes. Ultimately, there need to be some basic agreements about *what, how,* and *when* subjects or skills and attitudes are taught to solve problems of inequity in student outcomes. These decisions, and how they are implemented, become a system. A system is needed to promote consistency in standards and to ensure that best practice, as identified by research and school-based results, becomes standard practice for all teachers across the school.

A full fishbone diagram in our hypothetical case might look like Figure 8.6. Inevitably, there will be cross-over between causal factors. For example, in Figure 8.6, the fact that teaching methods vary from class to class might be attributed to teachers having different experiences in professional learning, or it might be because there is no documented "best practice" available to guide teachers, or both. These diagrams tend to get messy, as arrows need to connect different ideas—which is why it is useful to do this exercise on a whiteboard.

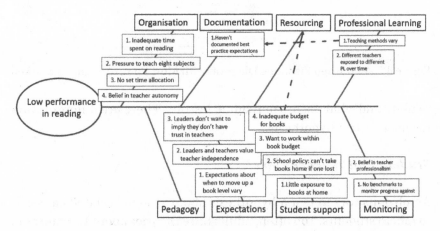

Figure 8.6. A Finished Fishbone Diagram

At this stage, it is beneficial to review the whole diagram to consider what the most powerful causes are and which ones should be addressed first. These can be circled or marked in some way, such as in Figure 8.7, before moving onto the next step in the process.

Checking Validity of Hypothesised Causes

It is important to check the validity of hypotheses in the fishbone diagram, not just assume their correctness. In the case about reading, having a review of the actual practices occurring in the classroom would validate (or invalidate) the theories about the processes that are occurring in the school, such as the amount of time spent on

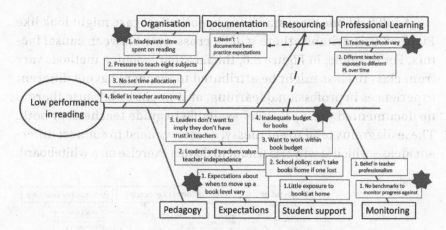

Figure 8.7. A Finished Fishbone Diagram with Most Powerful Causes Marked

reading and what occurs in reading lessons. There are different ways to check or test hypotheses.

Student and Teacher Voice

An obvious way to test a hypothesis about student-related causes is to talk to students. Too often, adults have theories about the causes of problems such as "lack of student engagement". This is a huge leap. On what basis can such a claim be made? When this theory was tested in one school by the principal talking to a group of boys who were not achieving well in written language, he found they were not disengaged. They liked writing. They just did not have the requisite skills. The reason for poor written language results was not the lack of student engagement or motivation, but the school's lack of a coherent and robust approach to teaching and monitoring the development of these skills. This is a good example of the need to look at the school as a system instead of looking at students or teachers as the source of the problem. Student voice helps to reveal or confirm the causes of underachievement.

Similarly, teachers often know the reason for underachievement, but leaders have not tapped into that knowledge. Teachers are usually very honest about any lack of confidence or knowledge gaps that they experience. Insights can be gained by discussion in groups of teachers in staff meetings. Asking for group feedback makes sampling teacher opinion about possible causes and solutions safe for individual teachers.

Quick Surveys

Alternately, quick, anonymous surveys can be used to check teacher or student views to validate or dismiss a hypothesis about the cause of a problem. For example, if there is a specific theory such as "teachers lack confidence in strategies to teach reading", it can be tested by asking "How confident are you in your knowledge of effective teaching strategies for reading comprehension?" with teachers rating their confidence as *Very strong, Strong, Moderate, Low, Very Low*. A graph of results provides the evidence as to whether the theory is supported.

Accessing Experts

While teachers may be confident in their teaching strategies, their confidence may not be well founded. Here, an external expert can be useful in providing an impartial review of organisational practices and teacher knowledge. For example, in one primary school the principal engaged an expert in written language to observe all teachers and to debrief teams of teachers on the positive and negative patterns they observed. In this way, the review was not personalised to each teacher, but focused on the strengths and weaknesses of teacher practice of groups of teachers. The findings from across the school were compiled, and this overview helped all staff to understand what needed to change to get improved results. The expert also recommended changes in organisational practices to strengthen the school's teaching of written language.

Theorising about Appropriate Strategies

The next step involves converting the fishbone diagram into a simple plan to address the causes. There are two common ways of doing this. First, the simplest way of mapping a theory of improvement is a Cause-Strategy Chart. Second, the traditional way of capturing the theory for improvement is a Driver Diagram.

Cause-Strategy Chart

In a Cause-Strategy Chart, such as Table 8.1, the hypothesised causes from the fishbone diagram are captured in column one; a way of checking the validity of this cause is noted in column two; and a solution strategy that addresses the identified causes is captured in column three. The chart maps out what changes need to occur in professional development, resourcing, expectations, documentation, pedagogy, and the organisation of the school, to address the causes of underachievement and see improvement. In the primary school example described, the leaders theorised that they needed to (1) allocate more funding to replenishing books each year; (2) develop clear expectations about core pedagogical practices that could be considered best practice; (3) decide on the amount of direct instruction students should receive; (4) establish some benchmarks for expected reading progress to monitor against; and (5) contract in expert help to provide professional development to improve pedagogical practices. Mapping strategies to causes in the fishbone diagram helps ensure that schools address all potential causes that are within their control, rather than having random spurts of activity. However, the details of these strategies still need to be fleshed out.

Driver Diagrams

A second approach to fleshing out a theory for improvement is facilitated by developing a *driver diagram*. In the driver diagram depicted in Figure 8.8, the problem *poor reading achievement* is turned into a measurable and challenging but potentially achievable target: *Improve reading levels across the school from 30% of students meeting national benchmarks to 60%.* The next column provides the primary drivers that are the main areas of concern that need to be addressed, as identified in the fishbone.

Table 8.1. Cause-Strategy Chart

Hypothesis/ Cause	Rationale/ evidence	Strategy
1. Inadequate budget for books	Teachers' voice	**Resourcing:** Increase reading budget to ensure that book stocks are replenished every year.
2. Expectations of reading progress vary because no set benchmarks	Teachers' voice Leaders' reflection	**Establish Standards:** Experts engaged to help set standards in discussion with teachers, based on national benchmarks that are generally achieved.
3. Time spent on direct instruction of reading may not be adequate	Teachers' voice Expert input	**Changes in Organisation:** Agree on number and duration of direct instructional sessions students should receive per week as optimal practice at different levels of the school.
4. No benchmarks to monitor student progress against	Expert input	**Develop benchmarks and monitor:** Monitor all junior students' progress against benchmarks every 5 weeks.
5. Teaching methods vary from class to class	Teachers' voice Expert input	**Professional Learning/Changes in Pedagogy:** Expert contracted to provide feedback on current approach and provide professional development to address pedagogical needs.

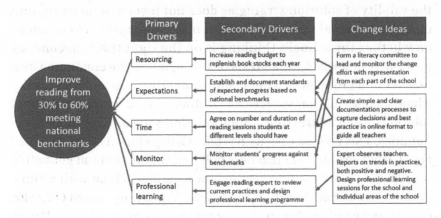

Figure 8.8. Driver Diagram

The overarching strategies are provided in the next column of boxes, which are referred to as the *Secondary Drivers*. In the third column, called *Change Ideas*, the change strategies are broken down into practical, short-term actions. Driver diagrams provide a plan to achieve a goal in a highly visible way that can be co-constructed with teachers. Once constructed, the theory for improvement becomes a work in progress, open to amendments. It may be visibly displayed in a staff room so that the improvement theory is transparent for all to see.

When thinking about strategies, there should always be a monitoring strategy. Typically, teachers and leaders overlook that a lack of robust, short-term monitoring on the part of the leadership team contributes to getting the current outcomes. Monitoring short-term outcomes or quick wins is probably the most powerful change behaviour that can be put in place. As soon as something is measured, people attend to it.

Checking Validity of Hypothesised Solutions

The validity of the thinking about solutions also needs to be checked. There are different ways of approaching this. First, experts are the obvious source for providing information on how to respond to specific pedagogical or organisational issues. The process of checking the validity of solution strategies does not involve schools signing up to professional development, but in asking experts to comment on whether the school's thinking is on the right track. Second, as previously described, small tests of strategies can be conducted by a teacher or a group of teachers before adopting solutions across the whole school. Another source can be other schools which have tested solutions when addressing similar problems in similar school communities. This was the case with Monet College (discussed in Chapter Four). Once leaders and teachers believed that they could get better results, they were open to seeing how a similar school with a similar problem had achieved improvement. Thus, they visited O'Keeffe College and were briefed on all their systems. As reported to us, Monet adopted O'Keeffe's systems "lock, stock, and barrel". Thus, the success of that approach was validated within a similar school community. In that example, the sources of the issues were in systems that the schools were missing. When systems were developed to monitor outcomes in the short term, and improvement cycles were engaged in, results improved. And they continued to improve each year.

Prioritising and Timelining Strategies

When there are a lot of possible strategies that seem to be worthwhile implementing, it is wise to prioritise and map out a timeline for implementing them. One commonly used technique for prioritising is to use quadrants to map strategies against their ease of implementation versus their impact, as in Figure 8.9.

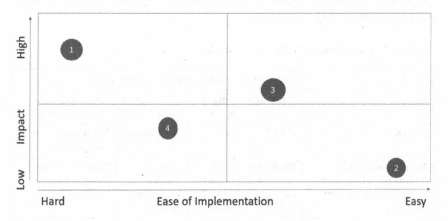

Figure 8.9. Impact Versus Ease Graph

The first priority is the strategy in the top right quartile; strategies in that quadrant are easy to execute and likely to have a high impact. The second priority is the strategy or the strategies in the top left quartile; these are more difficult to implement, but they still have a high impact. If a strategy is easy to implement but not likely to greatly impact outcomes, the school needs to consider whether the effort is worthwhile. Teachers and leaders will be more motivated if they are not over-burdened and if they see a notable short-term impact. However, it is frequently easy to see from a scan of the fishbone diagram which strategy fits into the quadrant of high impact and relative ease of implementation. Other criteria may also be important in deciding on which strategies to implement. For example, a school might have a great solution, but it is far too costly to be realistic to implement.

Once strategies are decided, they need to be time-lined in a formal improvement plan. This plan includes the pursuit of pedagogical quick wins and system strategies, as described in Chapter Four. A simple format to record a time-lined improvement plan is shown in Table 8.2. Essentially, this is the school's annual plan. It is a simple document of one or two pages per goal, and usually, schools should only pursue one priority academic goal at a time. Schools update the plan at the end of each cycle, or each school term based on their *refine and check* step of the cycle.

Table 8.2. A Time-lined Improvement Plan

Goal	To improve reading comprehension levels		
Target	Improve reading levels across the school, from 30% meeting national benchmarks to 60% by year's end.		
What?	**Why?**	**By When?**	**Who will make it happen?**
Measure quick wins (QW) and collate and report results at staff meeting	Each of the three areas of the school pursue QWs specific to their year level	Every 5 weeks, beginning Week 10	Leaders of the Junior/ middle / senior school
Provide clear guidance on number of instructional sessions students should receive in reading and other subjects	Large variation in practice across the school Teachers unclear on priorities	End of Week 4	Expert and senior leaders
Research and enact a set of expectations about year-by-year progress in junior years	No clear expectations about rate of progress	End of Week 4	Expert and senior leaders
Review current pedagogical practices and create a clear system of agreed-upon best practice micro-processes in reading	To create a best practice pedagogical guideline for teachers To guide input of professional learning programme	End of Week 10	External expert with senior leadership team and one representative from junior/ middle/senior teachers

The various types of strategies will be elaborated on in more depth in the next chapter. It should be noted that, while we outlined how to develop a plan for improvement in this chapter, often strategies emerge in the process of doing the improvement work. Many successful medical practices have been developed in this way. We learn by doing. That is a central mantra of the improvement cycle approach. Strategies will be tweaked as evidence from student data is examined and reacted to.

Key Points

- Using a tool such as the fishbone diagram is one way of supporting divergent thinking about causes.
- Strategies are planned to address causes. These can be mapped out in a Cause-Strategy chart or in a Driver Diagram.
- Strategies that are likely to be high impact and relatively easy to implement should be prioritised.
- Theories, both about causes and about solutions, need to be checked for validity.
- Some strategies emerge from what is learnt and are not pre-planned.

CHAPTER NINE

Implementing Strategies

In this chapter, we discuss different types of improvement strategies. They include communication; organisation and resourcing; professional learning; expectations and standardisation; documentation; and, finally, measuring and monitoring. We highlight common pitfalls in implementing these strategies and point to ways to effectively implement them.

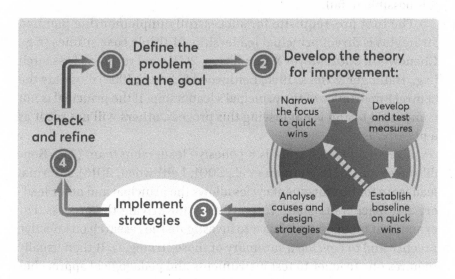

Figure 9.1. The School Improvement Cycle: Implement Strategies

Planning the initial school improvement cycle takes time, but once the first one or two test cycles have been undertaken to check the efficacy of the measurement tool and to develop the theory for improvement, the next steps of implementing strategies and reviewing results becomes more straightforward. Each subsequent cycle usually results in tweaks to improve measures or strategies. While earlier chapters focused on the development of improvement strategies and the testing of measurement tools, this chapter focuses on the implementation of the strategies chosen to bring about improvement. "Testing is about learning if the change will result in an improvement, and implementation is about how to make the change an integral part of the system" (Langley et al., 2009, p. 173).

What Are the Pre-requisites for Successful Implementation?

There are a number of pre-requisites for successful implementation. Even if a school has tested its measurement tool and developed a clear theory for improvement, without putting some pre-requisites in place it is possible to fail.

The first pre-requisite for successfully implementing planned strategies is direct principal leadership. Multiple case studies (e.g., Chenoweth, 2007; Meyer & Bendikson, 2021) and reviews of research (e.g., Hallinger & Heck, 1996; Leithwood & Jantzi, 1999) illustrate the central importance of the principal's leadership. If the principal is not committed to and is not driving this process, others will not see it as a priority.

A second pre-requisite is a cohesive leadership team (e.g., Bendikson et al., 2020; Hofman et al., 2001; Leithwood, 2016). A formal lead team for improvement cycles allows the principal and other leaders and teachers to share responsibility for driving the process. For example, it takes an enthusiast to investigate the research on effective practice and to develop a summary of those strategies. It then usually requires one teacher to test instruments and pedagogical approaches with a group of students. Someone needs to drive the overall process; this is usually the principal or a deputy principal with the very visible and enthusiastic sponsorship of the principal. Leading improvement is too big a job, even in small schools, for one person to do it all.

Third, routine meetings to lead improvement are essential. If the improvement cycle is not enacted through routine meetings, this approach will not take root. This is where leaders and teachers review student data which, in turn, drive decisions about changes to pedagogical and organisational practices. These meetings must become a strict routine.

Finally, there is a risk of the over-enthusiastic leader trying to go too big and broad, too soon. Thus, a final pre-requisite is keeping the degree of change manageable. We have advocated starting with small tests, learning, and spreading the messages of success initially. If what is advocated is a small change, it will be readily picked up by teachers. If, on the other hand, the changes advocated are very burdensome and do not have a short-term, strong and visible impact, teachers will not be helped to teach more effectively, which is the ultimate aim. Is the change good for students? Is it viable for teachers? If those two criteria are met, success is pretty well assured. Next, we outline types of strategies that are typically part of the repertoire of improving schools.

Types of Strategies

The types of strategies that tend to be required to implement improvement cycles fall into six main categories. They are: communication, organisation and resourcing, professional learning, expectations and standardisation, documentation, and measuring and monitoring.

Communication

The importance of communicating well is often underestimated in educational settings. Leaders have to be effective communicators to reach their goals and bring others with them. To do this, leaders must first build problem awareness, then progressively move to building goal and target awareness, and then to involving teachers and students in decisions and actions (Langley et al., 2009).

First, leaders have to create the will in others to pursue an improvement. Other leaders and teachers need to be able to see the reason for change or "the why" very clearly. Leaders build dissatisfaction with the old state without blaming anyone for it, and then help to paint a picture of the desired state. As illustrated in Chapter Four, this is often achieved by illustrating the high-level limiting factor in a clear graph, perhaps showing that the school is underperforming compared to similar schools or compared to its own earlier performance. The reason for having a goal should be clear and convincing to all.

It is also essential to show how any proposed change fits with the philosophy and longer-term direction of the school. A direct line should be able to be drawn between the vision, the goal, the target, the quick wins, and the other organisational changes that are being made. If the goal is clear, the desired state is clear, and this is what needs to be communicated. This clarity of purpose does not occur by having just one meeting. It is an ongoing process. Some principals create a PowerPoint that captures the "why" of the change, the clear goal and target, and the current focus of a meeting such as reporting back on or analysing quick-win data. In this way, the overarching purpose and process of what is occurring are briefly put before teachers repeatedly.

Some schools we have worked with have found it useful to create a *plan on a page* to create this clarity. On one page they state the problem, the goal, the target, the initial quick wins, and the three or so major strategies that are being employed to realise the goal. Having this artefact up around the school then helps to reinforce the goal focus and maintain clarity about what a school is trying to achieve and how they are trying to achieve it. Of course, equally, such an artefact could be created and have no impact on the clarity of goal direction if, for example, there was no living proof of the plan on a page being pursued in the real, day-to-day life of teachers or students. Nothing undermines leadership more than failing to "walk the talk".

Second, having created the will to improve, the leader's role is to clearly make decisions based on results of quick wins. Leaders graph results and openly discuss the good and bad with teachers without blame, but with a theorising and problem-solving mindset. Leaders model the mindset of acting on evidence of what is effective. If the quick-win results are not evident, the question has to be asked, "What has gone wrong? Have the agreed pedagogical strategies not been applied? Have the strategies worked with some students but not with others?" Leaders acknowledge and address negative or inadequate impacts openly, although, if testing has been done, negative impacts should be rare.

Third, leaders express confidence in those who implement the strategies, whether they are teachers or leaders. When starting out on a new strategy, everyone involved can feel a sense of risk. "What if this does not work? What if the results aren't what we hope for?" These are natural fears, given that the school has invested so much time and effort to change their approach to improvement and implement improvement cycles. It is important to stress that this is an ongoing, problem-solving exercise. Mistakes will be made, but everyone is learning to be better teachers and leaders, and students will be the beneficiaries of this learning.

Organisation and Resourcing

Not all changes require a formal cycle. Sometimes extra resources are required, and improvement can be quickly achieved by changing the roles of some people or by prioritising spending to support the work toward the goal focus. For example, one school changed the role of a teacher to provide extra tuition at a particular level of the school. Another school made changes to the number of lessons students received in a week. These simple changes had a large impact.

Similarly, many organisational changes can be put in place, and their positive impact is quickly evident. First on the list of organisational changes is usually a change to meeting structures in schools. In Gauguin Primary's case (Chapter Two), the principal emphasised that none of the processes they embedded could have occurred without fundamentally changing the way teachers were grouped and regularly met. This organisational change was quickly recognised as a positive change by teachers. In a secondary school in particular, this type of approach can be difficult to facilitate when there are limited meeting times available, usually due to teachers having contracted "maximum contact hours". It takes commitment to find the best meeting structures. Teachers usually re-purpose their scheduled meetings.

Another level of meetings is required, though, which was well-illustrated by O'Keeffe College in Chapter Three. The senior leaders had a number of their own meetings to drive the improvement process with heads of faculty. These meetings, when run in focused ways, ensure that there is collective accountability—in other words, everyone is accountable to everyone else. The senior leaders have to follow through on their commitment to help solve any problems the head of faculty is experiencing, just as the head of faculty is accountable for improving student outcomes. The school's goal is front of mind for everyone.

To keep this focus and accountability, there can be no cancelled meetings. Monet High's senior leaders (discussed in Chapter Four), reported that none of them ever missed one of their weekly meetings. Every week, the principal and the two deputy principals met with a year-level leader to review results and to decide on follow-up actions. These meetings were on a 3-week cycle, and every meeting finished with actions for either senior leaders or the year-level leader to achieve before the next meeting. Sometimes these involved following up with certain teachers or students. These meetings provided senior leaders with the intimate and up-to-date details of how each student was progressing and provided them with the opportunity to reinforce positive results of some of the more challenged students when they met them around the school. Their personal knowledge of each student's progress helped to motivate both teachers and students.

Because the roles of senior and middle leaders are so fundamental to driving the improvement, the job descriptions and expectations for people in these roles usually have to change. Often, middle leaders have a largely administrative role. When schools move to the improvement cycle approach, their instructional role for staff becomes critical. Those responsibilities and expectations need to be explained, along with why they are so important.

Professional Learning

In most of the case study schools referred to in this book, one of the senior leaders' first moves was to support the development of the instructional leadership skills of middle leaders. There are many fundamental leadership skills that teachers need to learn to become effective leaders. All middle leaders should understand some basic leadership theory to enable their self-reflection and ability to build an effective team. In addition, practical skills are required of people in these key positions, including how to run a meeting, how to do some basic analysis of student performance data, and how to build trust in teams. These skills need to be learnt, and middle leaders need time and money invested in them for this to occur, because this usually requires the engagement of an outside provider. This can occur simultaneously as the first cycles are undertaken.

Most of the professional learning for teachers occurs at professional learning meetings, either at the team level, where quick-win data are examined, or at the whole-staff meeting, where process measures and quick-win results are examined and discussed. For example, a process measure may be that each team presents one slide about how they have implemented the planned pedagogical change. The quick-win data would be their interim results from students. The review and discussion of these, and what impact they are seeing to date, prompts the professional learning across teams. For instance, one team's practices may be more successful than those of others. The learning comes from what is making it more successful. Or one team may have tweaked the agreed pedagogical changes in some way that other teams agree is more effective. This can prompt a change to all of their practices in the next cycle.

Effective professional learning can also be delivered by a provider, either an expert from within the school or from external partners. Once gaps in teacher knowledge or skills are identified, some "front-loading" of content or pedagogical knowledge or skills may be appropriate. Many schools find it more effective to save up their one allotted hour of professional development per week into a 2- or 3-hour block so they can deeply engage with teachers in new and relevant learning.

Professional learning is effective when certain conditions are met (Timperley et al., 2007). One is that teachers are absolutely clear on what they are trying to achieve through the learning. This is facilitated by being clear on the problem as illustrated in the long-term outcome data that are usually only available annually (lag data), and then making very overt connections to the teacher learning and the results in the quick-win data. Further, the professional learning needs to focus not just on what teachers should do, but also the theory about *why* this is going to be more effective. Teachers need to be clear on that rationale for any changes they make to their practice. They do not benefit from blindly following recipes for good teaching but, rather, from understanding why a practice is effective. This learning requires multiple opportunities to engage with theory and to review the results from their changed practice. No change in pedagogical practices will be sustained unless teachers see that the changed practice is more effective than the old practice, and they understand why. This requires that the leader of the professional development has the content knowledge and pedagogical expertise to successfully engage with the teachers. It may be a leader from within the school or an external expert, but it has to be someone who has a level of expertise that provides them with confidence to openly engage with teachers' theories about what is effective and what is not. Sometimes, internal experts can be reluctant to challenge the practices or theories of teachers because they do not want to risk their relationships with their colleagues. Thus, external experts can be very useful in driving the change process, not only because of their depth of content knowledge but also because they can legitimise or support the leadership of the principal. The support shows that "This is not just some whim; it is proven effective practice".

Finally, principals should be active participants in the professional learning with the teachers. They need to be able to engage with the teachers during their learning and be able to respond to any challenges that arise. This active engagement communicates the importance of the professional learning, shows support for teachers, and enables early identification of barriers for implementing the new learning.

Expectations and Standardisation

Almost inevitably, changes in expectations and some standardisation of practices are part of an improvement effort because, often, the reasons for a slip in performance include the lack of a standard, together with the lack of a coherent approach to reaching that standard.

Standards for student performance reflect expectations—high or low. Frequently, staff are unaware of how their students are performing, because they are not provided with any benchmark against which to review their standards. Relatively low performance can be readily accepted as normal due to beliefs about students' ability or teachers' beliefs about the impact of societal poverty. Or, in relatively high-performing schools in high socioeconomic areas, a school's underperformance can be hidden by face-value results that look good, even if the school is not adding great value year-to-year.

Teacher and student beliefs about their potential to perform affect what effort goes into improvement by both teachers and students. When teachers believe that learners are unlikely to perform well, or are likely to perform highly, they interact with the students in ways that convey those beliefs. When students see that teachers believe they can achieve, their self-belief is driven up, and they work harder to achieve. But when teachers convey their lack of belief in students to succeed, the students assimilate that belief (Rubie-Davies, 2015). Teachers impact the results of their whole classes with these beliefs, not just the students who may be performing at lower levels. Teachers with high expectations accelerate all students' progress regardless of their starting point, and because they believe in the ability of all students to achieve, they work hard to achieve results. Teachers without that belief, however, have little reason to extend themselves in their efforts for students.

There are three key ways that high-expectation teachers' practices differ from those of low-expectation teachers (Rubie-Davies, 2015). The first is class climate: high-expectation teachers create a warm, supportive environment for all learners. All students are expected to respect and support others to learn. The second is goal setting: high-expectation teachers set new learning goals for students regularly. These are their quick wins. The third is grouping practices: high-expectation teachers use flexible grouping practices. At times, the whole class is taught, at times students with similar skill levels or a lack in a particular skill are pulled together in a group and, at other times, students with similar interests might work together. These teachers do not have fixed *ability groups*. The very name *ability group* indicates a belief that some students are smarter than others, rather than that all students can learn. Ability grouping maintains the status quo. The students who start in the bottom group in their first year of primary or secondary school usually remain there for the rest of their schooling. Ability grouping and *streaming* (ability grouping whole classes) in secondary schools is a dominant practice in Australasian schools and is one of the reasons why we have the least equitable schooling results in the world (Schmidt et al., 2015). Our schools often exacerbate inequity rather than address it, by trying to differentiate. High-expectation classes differentiate less, not more. All students are given the opportunity to choose tasks and to engage in high-level learning activities regardless of their levels of prior learning.

This idea is captured by the notion of *opportunities to learn*. Students can only learn if they are exposed to the content and skills they require and provided with the opportunity to practise them. Students who are in low-ability groups or streamed classes are more likely to be students from ethnic minority groups or from lower socio-economic backgrounds. These students get exposed to fewer opportunities to learn and less engaging activities and, as a consequence, the gap between their performance and that of other students grows. It is called the "Matthew effect of accumulated advantage": the rich get richer and the poor get poorer.

All teachers' performance can be improved and become more consistent when optimal practices for teachers and leaders are standardised. These practices can be thought of as macro- and micro-processes that are developed through both expert input and testing of ideas in cycles (Bryk et al., 2015). Macro-processes are processes made up from micro-processes. The example that Bryk and colleagues use is that macro-processes in literacy are interactive read aloud; shared reading; interactive writers' workshops; word study; and guided reading. These macro-processes are agreed-upon approaches to teaching reading and writing. Each of the approaches is made up of micro-processes. Guided reading, for example, is made up of the following standard micro-processes: teachers select a text; introduce a text; engage students in conversation about the topic; students read independently;

teachers engage students about the meaning of the text; and teachers conclude with a teaching point about specific reading strategies targeted in the lesson. In other words, in a school, standardisation occurs in a subject area by agreeing on the core parts of the course or subject and the best practices that they entail. The discussion and agreement about these processes lead to greater coherence in a school and the secure knowledge that every teacher is teaching agreed-upon core elements.

When schools do not have some agreed-upon standard processes, a belief in teacher autonomy is sometimes cited as the reason. Every class is different, and every teacher should have the ability to be creative in their approach to teaching—but that idea does not conflict with the need for every teacher to use the processes that are demonstrably most effective. Just as every surgeon does not carry out an operation *their* way, neither should every teacher carry out their teaching role by disregarding the evidence about the most effective practices. It is the leaders' role to bring in the expertise and evidence to highlight best practice and the reasons why it is effective. Its effectiveness should further be evidenced by the quick-win data. Teachers' discussion and agreement about core macro- and micro-processes help to create deeper and more consistent knowledge across teachers and more coherence across the teaching in the school. This coherence enhances learning for all students because of the consistency of messages and approaches.

Documentation

Any expectations and agreements about teaching content, processes, or data management need to be captured in a school's documentation so that teachers can refer to it for guidance. This also helps to manage the inevitable changes to staffing and the need to induct new staff into the agreed practices as time goes on. The coherence and clarity these documents create improve the consistency of the quality of teaching across a school or department. One example of the benefits is described by Chenoweth (2007), who cites one school's curriculum maps:

The core of helping children learn at East Millsboro is instruction, and instruction begins with the school's "curriculum maps". The curriculum map is a document developed by East Millsboro teachers working together in grade level teams to map out, month by month, what they will be teaching. It is drawn in part from state standards and contains performance indicators students must meet during the month, plus essential questions, skills, assessments specialized vocabulary, and texts to be used to teach that unit. . . . As a result of the curriculum map, even teachers new to East Millsboro have clearly laid out guidelines for what their instruction must include. (p. 156)

Artefacts, or smart tools, also help to create clarity and consistency and are often created to help embed strategies. We have already referred to examples such as a plan on a page, a meeting template, or a curriculum map. Artefacts can also assist coherent teaching and monitoring processes in the classroom in the form of a rubric to assist monitoring, or a poster showing the main parts of a strategy for students, such as the "PEEL" strategy for writing a paragraph, illustrated in Figure 9.2. Artefacts help to embed strategies and create greater coherence which, in turn, increase the chance of school improvement because teachers and students across the school are getting a consistent message.

Measuring and Monitoring

The need for effective routines to measure quick-win outcomes and to create tables and graphs of data to communicate those results has been a feature of this book. There is no improvement cycle if there is not the regular measurement and monitoring of quick wins for students. This requires strict meeting routines and the ability to create graphs and tables to communicate results, and to take action on the basis of that information. Details about this will be explored in Chapter Ten.

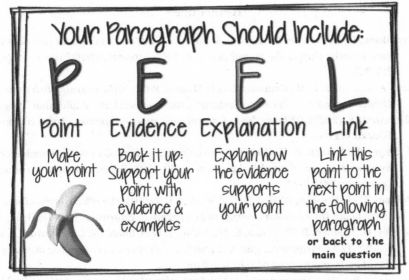

Figure 9.2. A Poster Illustrating an Agreed Strategy: An Example of an Artefact

Key Points

- Implementing strategies is different from testing tools and strategies to see if they work, which is done initially as the lead team builds the theory for improvement.
- Implementation requires systems and processes to be put in place to sustain agreed changes that improve teaching and learning.
- To be successful, strong principal leadership is required, along with a dedicated "lead team", which usually encompasses middle leaders or enthusiastic teachers.
- Most of the work is accomplished through the efficient and focused use of routine meetings.
- Implementing effective strategies creates better results for students by enhancing teaching and organisational effectiveness and coherence.
- Professional learning needs to be focussed, to challenge existing theories, and be actively supported by the principal.

References

Bendikson, L., Broadwith, M., Zhu, T., & Meyer, F. (2020). Goal pursuit practices in high schools: Hitting the target? *Journal of Educational Administration, 58*(6), 713–728.

Bryk, A. S., Gomez, L. M., Grunow, A., & LeMahieu, P. G. (2015). *Learning to improve: How America's schools can get better at getting better.* Harvard Education Press.

Chenoweth, K. (2007). *It's being done: Academic success in unexpected schools.* Harvard Education Press.

Hallinger, P., & Heck, R. H. (1996). Reassessing the principal's role in school effectiveness: A review of empirical research, 1980–1995. *Education Administration Quarterly, 32*(1), 5–44.

Hofman, R. H., Hofman, W. H. A., & Guldemond, H. (2001). The effectiveness of cohesive schools. *International Journal of Leadership in Education, 4*(2), 115–135.

Langley, G. J., Moen, R. D., Nolan, K. M., Nolan, T. W., Clifford, N. L., & Provost, L. P. (2009). *The improvement guide: A practical approach to enhancing organizational performance* (2nd ed.). Jossey-Bass.

Leithwood, K. (2016). Department-head leadership for school improvement. *Leadership and Policy in Schools, 15*(2), 117–140.

Leithwood, K., & Jantzi, D. (1999). Transformational school leadership effects: A replication. *School Effectiveness and School Improvement, 10*(4), 451–479.

Meyer, F., & Bendikson, L. (2021). Improving gender equity in written language. In D. Peterson & S. P. Carlile (Eds.), *Improvement Science: Promoting equity in schools.* Meyers Education Press.

Rubie-Davies, C. M. (2015). *Becoming a high expectation teacher.* Routledge.

Schmidt, W. H., Burroughs, N. A., Zoido, P., & Houang, R. T. (2015). The role of schooling in perpetuating educational inequality: An international perspective. *Educational Researcher, 44*(7), 371–386.

Timperley, H., Wilson, A., Barrar, H., & Fung, I. (2007). *Teacher professional learning and development.* Ministry of Education.

CHAPTER TEN

Checking and Refining

In this chapter, we discuss how a leadership team checks that the implemented changes have resulted in improvement and refines their improvement theory as a result of these checks. As Hinnant-Crawford (2020) points out, "There are two major tasks within the improvement science process: discovering or developing improvements and then determining if the improvements work" (p. 36).

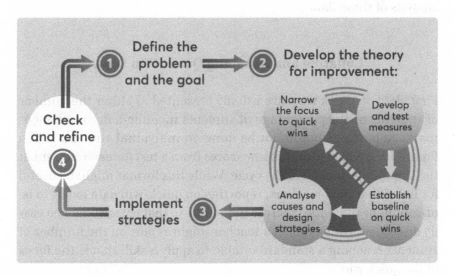

Figure 10.1. The School Improvement Cycle: Check and Refine

Determining the extent to which the predicted improvement has occurred, and then reacting to that by refining the next steps in light of the results, is critical. Checking occurs at two levels. First, lead indicators are used at the end of each cycle. The lead indicators are the measures of the quick wins of students and the process data that inform the leadership team of the extent to which teachers have implemented the agreed-upon changes. Second, improvement across the school is determined by checking lag indicators at the end of a year in a school. They provide big-picture trends. These data are the ultimate test of the validity of a school's theory for improvement, allowing schools to answer the questions: "Did the changes we made result in improved outcomes? Have we met our target for the year?"

Collating and presenting the data on lead indicators and, in particular, lag indicators, in order to check progress is the responsibility of the leadership team, although this responsibility may be delegated to others. Whoever does it needs to be aware of certain protocols in presenting the data. Unless the data are well presented, it is challenging to decide if any improvement has been made. In this chapter, we thus provide some guidance on collating and graphing to support analysis of these data.

Collating and Graphing Quick-Win Data

First, data on quick wins are usually presented as either the number of students or the percentage of students meeting a desired benchmark. Reporting should not be done on individual students, as in Figure 10.2, which presents raw scores from a test for each student at the beginning and end of the cycle. While this format might be useful for individual class teachers, reporting on quick-win data needs to be on groups of students or across the school so that patterns can be easily discerned. For example, a teacher might report on the number of students reaching a standard or able to apply a skill that is the focus of the quick win.

Further, when a teacher is dealing with raw scores from a test, such as in Figure 10.3, averages are rarely a useful format for reporting quick-win data, because quick wins focus on discrete skills that are mastered (or not), unlike "tests" that produce raw scores that usually provide feedback on multiple items and skills in a collated format. Tests can be used for quick wins, but there must be a way of recording the mastery of concepts or skills for a quick win. For example, if there were 10 test items all focusing on place value, three or four

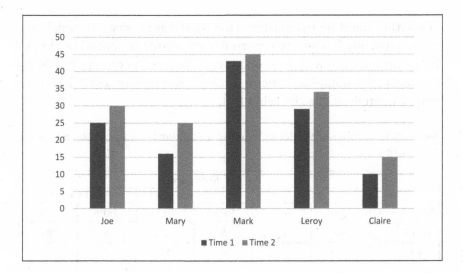

Figure 10.2. Student-by-Student Spelling Assessment Raw Scores

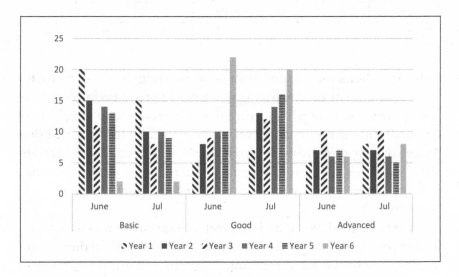

Figure 10.3. Number of Students Meeting Basic, Good, and Advanced Standards in Sentence Construction

concepts would likely be assessed, such as: ability to count objects to 10, ability to name one more and one less than a number between 10 and 20, and ability to name one more or one less than a number between 20 and 30. Thus, a raw score will not be as helpful as a record of whether the students mastered the three key concepts tested. More commonly, quick wins are reported from results of rubrics or checklists that indicate whether, or to what degree, a concept has been mastered, a standard or benchmark has been met, or a skill has been demonstrated, such as in Table 10.1.

Table 10.1. Number of Students Meeting a Standard in a Rubric on Sentence Structure

	Standard					
	Basic		Good		Advanced	
Year Level	June	July	June	July	June	July
Year 1	20	15	5	7	5	8
Year 2	15	10	8	13	7	7
Year 3	11	8	9	12	10	10
Year 4	14	10	10	14	6	6
Year 5	13	9	10	16	7	5
Year 6	2	2	22	20	6	8

Table 10.1 shows the number of students meeting the set standard for each year level at the beginning and the end of the cycle. Year-level data provide more of a big picture than classroom level data if there are multiple classes at each level, and can be used to check whether there are huge discrepancies in one year level compared to others. For example, if one year level showed a lot more improvement than others, the school would want to investigate why, so all teachers could learn from it.

To check quick-win data for overall improvement and to communicate results to staff at this stage, data can be even further aggregated to a school level. Presenting data across year levels often does not provide a clear picture, as can be seen from Figure 10.3.

One either has to graph data for each year level or aggregate the data across the school to create a clearer picture for discussing school-wide trends. Aggregating means adding up the numbers of students at each year level to make a table such as Table 10.2, which depicts results for the whole school.

Table 10.2. Total Number of Students Meeting Standards in Sentence
Structure

Basic		Good		Advanced	
June	July	June	July	June	July
75	54	64	82	41	44

When Table 10.2 is converted into a graph, as in Figure 10.4, it is easy
to see the pattern across the school. The advantage of collating the
data at the school level is that it can be presented at a staff meeting
without "pointing the finger": at any one class or teacher, year level
team, or subject area. It creates a collective sense of how the school
is progressing and allows teachers to discuss the trends somewhat
dispassionately. Then teams of teachers can graph their own classes,
year level, or subject area results in the same way, so they can analyse
trends in their teaching teams and reflect on their impact on individual students or groups of students.

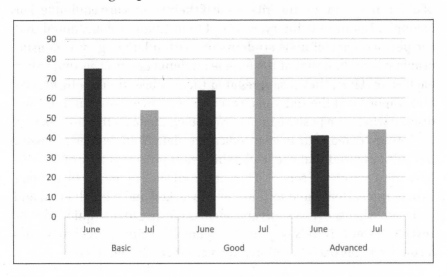

Figure 10.4. Number of Students Meeting Basic, Good, and Advanced
Standards in Sentence Construction

Second, another protocol may be around the degree to which the
school "cleans" the quick-win data. Clean data mean that students

are matched across the data set. For example, if new students have arrived since baseline data were collected, they would not be included in the next reporting of quick-win data. In that way, the staff can see the actual impact on the students who were there throughout the cycle. In the same way, if the data are clean, any student who left the school before data were collected at the end of the cycle would also be removed.

However, when showing the data on the next cycle, again, all students who were present for Time 1 (pre-cycle) and Time 2 (post-cycle) data collection would be included in the figures. Whether a school does this data cleaning or not is up to them, but, if the data on quick wins are not clear and there has been a lot of student movement in and out of the school, it is difficult to assess the impact of the strategy.

Third, while an aggregated view of the data is important to see the big picture for the school, it may be useful to examine disaggregated quick-win data. Disaggregation means to separate out the data of different groups of students to see if their results are equitable. For example, Bonnard Primary, referred to in Chapter Four, noted that the performance of male students in written language was considerably worse than that of the female students and was getting worse each year. Thus, they disaggregated their quick-win data by gender and graphed it at the end of each cycle to keep an eye on that trend and discern whether a positive impact was being made on the discrepancy.

Groups of teachers need to look at the data from their own classes, but it is essential that the leadership team pulls together quick-win data from across the school. This allows all staff to see the bigger picture of the patterns and to share what worked and what did not, and to decide what the next steps are, such as moving to new quick wins or revisiting some. In this way, across-school learning is facilitated, and a coherent approach to refining next steps can be agreed on.

Collating and Presenting Process Data

While collecting the quick-win data is largely the responsibility of individual teachers, and collating it is senior leadership's responsibility, the leadership team needs to both collect and collate the process data.

Did the teachers carry out the practices as they agreed? Collecting and collating these data are important; leaders need to know if improvement was not made because their theory about the quick wins was incorrect, or because teachers were inconsistent in the uptake of the agreed pedagogical strategy.

Process data are usually simple to collect, and several methods were outlined in Chapter Seven. To reiterate briefly, one of the most successful ways is to simply have teachers report back mid-cycle to a staff meeting on the strategy they are applying, what evidence of impact they have, and any potential challenges they face. Collecting these data mid-cycle means that everyone can benefit from the learning of others as soon as possible, and leaders can react if there are barriers to implementing the strategies. For example, each team might report back on: *What we did and what we noticed about the impact*; *What results we are seeing to date*; and *Implications for the next cycle*.

Another way of collecting process data is to observe teachers. At Gauguin Primary, whose case study featured in Chapter Two, the two deputy principals carried out regular, timetabled observations in classrooms. In that chapter, Table 2.4 from Gauguin Primary illustrates how they collated and presented data on observations and recommendations.

A third way to collect process data is to use videoed student feedback or by using surveys or small-group interviews. Short surveys can be completed online, or on paper, and can be anonymous to encourage students to be open and honest in their feedback. Students can be asked about their level of agreement with the changes or to write feedback, and both data can be collated and presented at a staff meeting, omitting any feedback that might point to an individual teacher or department.

Similarly, data on the extent of implementation of organisational changes can be collected from teachers and students, where applicable. For example, teachers can provide feedback on new meeting structures or the usefulness of templates and smart tools, and leaders can note whether these are actively used and benefit their work (and that of teachers) and ensure that positive changes are built into new routines.

What Are the Next Steps?

If the quick-win data do not show the results that might have been anticipated, either something is wrong with the theory for improvement, or something is wrong with the attempts to measure or implement the changes. If the process data indicate that teachers did faithfully implement what was agreed pedagogically, then questions can be raised about the theory for improvement, such as the following: Which pedagogical strategies worked and which did not? Were the planned changes realistic? Was the time frame long enough? For example, was the change too big to impact the quick-win outcome in the short period of time? Or was the school trying to achieve too much at once? Sometimes schools create a list of up to 10 quick wins and then try to pursue them all at once. This is unlikely to reap clear improvements. Schools have to have the courage to go slow on the quick wins and ensure that students are secure in one or two "basics" captured by the quick wins before moving onto the next one or two. Or, it may be that the quick-win skill was dependent on another skill that had been overlooked. For example, a school was testing students' ability to infer, but they found after one cycle that they needed to take a step back and teach students to locate important information from the text before they could infer. This meant that the next cycle was refined to teaching the pre-requisite skill of locating important information. Alternatively, questions could be asked of the measurement tool: Do we need more refinement in the measurement tool?

If almost all students succeed with the first quick win, the school or team moves onto the next quick win, remembering, of course, that this process works alongside business-as-usual teaching. It is a process of ensuring that all teachers in the team focus on teaching some basic skills at the same time, in the same way, and thereby improve all students' opportunties to learn more advanced skills. However, it is not the only thing teachers are teaching.

If the results of the quick win show that only some of the students have progressed, but there are still a large or moderate number of students who have not mastered the quick win, then the school may want to refine the next cycle by taking a "target student" approach and focusing in on those students for the quick win. Once most students have control of that quick win, a team of teachers can move onto the next quick win. Or, alternately, they can have a list of quick wins they want all students to achieve and have an individual target student approach, with each student having one or two personal goals at a time, as was the case with Gauguin Primary in Chapter Two.

Finally, improvement does not result from pedagogical changes alone. Organisational changes need to be embedded into systems so that improvements become part of the new way of working. Schools must not move onto another goal focus or quick win without ensuring the new routines are established to maintain the current gains. This often means that changes are required in curriculum plans to ensure that key sticking points for students are constantly revisited.

Collating and Graphing Lag Indicators

The review of the lag data is both the most exciting and the scariest time! Finally, a school sees if the theory for improvement really worked, and to what degree. But many schools seem overwhelmed by the amount of data they receive from their systems, and as a result they often do not attend closely enough to key indicators. However, being able to read school data is essential and becomes easier if it is clear what data is valued and what trends the school is watching carefully each year. When schools track the key indicators they really value, patterns over time become much more evident.

There are some protocols that should be adhered to when graphing data so that the picture presented is as good a replication of the "reality" of the students' results as possible. One is to have the Y (vertical) axis labelled 0 to 100 if using percentages, and to have it start from 0 if numbers are used; otherwise, the picture presented can be misleading.

For example, in Figure 10.5, the decline in scores looks dramatic, which may lead some people to think something major occurred, but when the Y axis is corrected to start from zero, the real perspective is evident.

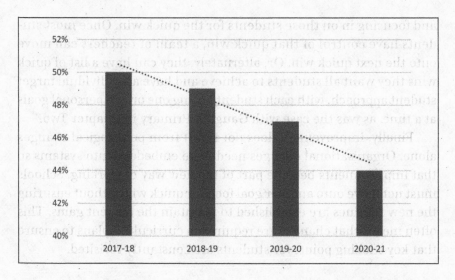

Figure 10.5. Graph with Faulty Y Axis for Percentages of Students Making More than 1 Year's Growth

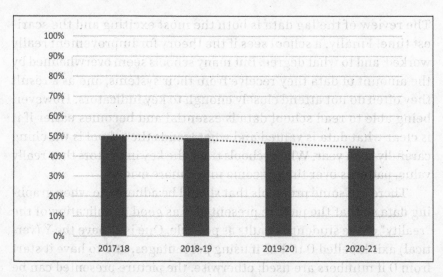

Figure 10.6. Graph with Correct Y Axis for Percentages of Students Making More Than 1 Year's Growth

As shown in Figure 10.6, the decline is real, but the degree of regression in the last period is more accurately depicted and not quite as dramatic as it first appeared when the axis was not following protocols. When comparing graphs, they should have the same axis values so an accurate comparison can readily be made.

Second, particularly when dealing with data that are not standardised, such as Overall Teacher Judgments commonly used in New Zealand, these ratings should be *triangulated* against some standardised data whenever possible. Triangulation involves checking the validity of one's data against other sources. Standardised tests are not the only source for triangulating. If in doubt about the validity of results, one could also check results from the day-to-day work of students or talk to students about their answers and get them to explain what they wrote for answers and why. Sometimes written language results, in particular, do not show the expected growth in the first year of using the school improvement cycle, but often that is because the teachers have become harder markers as they have come to understand the agreed standards better. It does not always mean students have not progressed.

Third, in contrast to quick-win data, it is generally not useful to clean lag data. The aim of reviewing these is to see how all students in the school performed in a given year. Having said that, it is useful to look at different cuts of the data to learn more about what is happening. For example, one school with very high student turnover tracked all the students who were enrolled in the school and stayed in the school, compared to the group who were transient. This provided them with a good indication of their effectiveness when students stayed at the school for their entire schooling. When reporting to their governing board, they reported on all students—those who had been in the school throughout, and those who had changed schools. These various cuts of data were not to make excuses but to inform decision making. When there are high levels of transience, a school must react strategically to that situation—for example, by quickly assessing students who enter the school and developing appropriate programmes to cater for them.

Fourth, the school needs to decide whether using percentages or numbers of students reaching a standard is the most meaningful way to present and examine data. For very small groups of students, only student numbers and names should be tracked, not percentages. Creating graphs with percentages adds nothing to the teachers' understanding when numbers of students are very small. Having both numbers and percentages in the data overview document is valuable. For larger groups, percentages are most useful for reporting trends but, when recording percentages, round the figures to make them more manageable. For example, with NCEA data, schools get results such as 86.7% of students passed a qualification. Round anything ending in a 5, 6, 7, 8, or 9, to the nearest 10, so 86.7% would become 87%, and 86.5% would become 87%, but 86.3% would become 86%.

A fifth protocol relates to disaggregation of data. It should be done as a matter of course to check that inequities in gender or ethnic groups are not apparent or that they are being addressed. When disaggregating data by ethnicity, it is recommended that a school review data for the main ethnic groups and any ethnic group that has a history of relative underperformance. It is important to not compare minority ethnic groups to "all students", because all students include that minority group, so it is not a valid comparison. Some schools have up to 50 ethnic groups. In that case, the predominant groups should be graphed along with any ethnic group for whom there is concern and any indigenous groups so that equity issues can be identified. When there are many ethnic groups that have only 5 or 10 students, which is often the case in large secondary schools with diverse student populations, these might be grouped together as "other ethnic groups". Further, students from similar ethnic groups—for example, Pacific Island students from a number of different islands—may be grouped together if numbers are small.

A sixth protocol is that schools should always compare their lag data to those of similar schools, if these data are available. This comparison is important, because regardless of how the data look on their own, by comparing outcomes to those of similar schools, a school can better judge its actual performance. Table 10.3 shows how to set these data out before graphing them. It can be useful to present these data by having the school's results in a bar graph and the comparable schools in a line such as is illustrated in Figure 10.7, or a different-coloured column could be used for comparison. This clearly shows how a school is performing compared to similar schools.

Finally, data need to be presented in formats that allow teachers to see trends. This might mean some data need to be grouped

Table 10.3. Percentage of Students Who Achieved the Qualification at
School A and to Similar Schools

	2020		2021	
Qualification	**Similar Schools**	**School A**	**Similar Schools**	**School A**
Year 11	88	95	90	85
Year 12	85	75	95	82
Year 13	80	89	76	84
UE	65	52	68	53

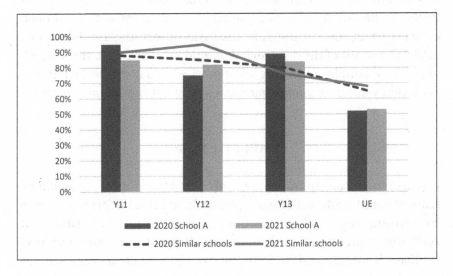

Figure 10.7. Percentage of Students Who Achieved the Qualification at School
A and Similar Schools

together to enable a bigger-picture view. For example, where results
are reported in six bands, a school might collate the data to show the
number or percentage of students scoring within bands one and two,
those scoring in bands three and four, and those scoring in bands five
and six. Or when scores are reported in stanines, it may be useful to
collate the data to show the number or percentage of students scoring at certain bands of stanines, such as stanines one to three, four
to six, and seven to nine, as these bands separate those considerably
below, at, or above average. Further, in secondary schools it is wise
to map the performance of each department in this way and to track

their performance over the years, as departments are "not uniformly effective" (Highfield, 2010, p. 173). Leadership teams need to monitor and support departments to become more effective. That is the purpose of reviewing these data.

Given the points above, some school leaders may feel they do not have the competency with spreadsheets to do this job. However, the level of competence required is not great. One simply needs to be able to draw up good tables of data, examples of which have been given in this chapter, and use these tables to create graphs. These tasks do not require any statistical knowledge. Differences between groups of students can be ascertained from the graphs and tables and do not need to be tested for statistical significance. Any observations and decisions made as a result of the data review should be recorded in the school's plan—for example, recording what worked, what did not, what was done that was not originally planned, and what should happen next.

Qualitative Data

It is also important to note the trends that are observed by teachers, students, and leaders. For example, with an initial effort to improve written language, a school may not see large shifts in the lag data, but staff might have positive observations. It is not uncommon to hear feedback from staff and students, for example, that teachers are more aware of what to teach and how to teach it, that teachers are more confident, or that students are more confident as writers. Similarly, teachers may report that the pedagogical changes are too hard to implement in some classes, or that the measurement tools are too time-consuming. These qualitative findings are equally important to gather, record, and react to in the next cycle.

Refining the Next Steps

Answering "what next?" depends on whether a school is reviewing quick-win data or lag data. If it is the former, changes are small and the results quickly assessed, so any failure to impact can be responded to readily. However, lag data are usually only available once a year and signal an opportunity to step back and consider the big picture: "Are we trying to solve the right problem? Are we being effective?" The critical test of the validity of the theory for improvement is the lag data. If lag data results are disappointing, but the quick-win data were showing that progress was being made, that suggests that the quick wins were not good predictors of the lag indicators, or it may be that the baseline was not accurate, as teachers became more proficient at judging standards over the course of the first year. It is time to go back to the fishbone diagram to aid this reflection and consider what is causing the problem and again consider "What needs to be changed to get a better result?"

A critical question to ask at this stage is: "Did the outcomes universally improve, or is there outcome variation? In other words, are some classes or groups of students mostly improving while others are not?" This is a key tenet of improvement science: learning from variation, not being dismayed by it. Teams need to ask themselves: "Why are some classes performing better than others? What is occurring that is different in those classes? Is it replicable?" Teachers invariably bring many different nuances to their teaching and, while teachers may make the agreed changes to their pedagogical practices, they will also make other changes that occur to them in the teaching moment. These unplanned but effective strategies that emerge in practice need to be captured as part of the next iteration of the theory for improvement. They are part of the new theory about what works, and they need to be tested in other classes.

Often, in the first year of taking an improvement cycle approach, results show an improvement, but not a large one. This is usually because the school has been pursuing the quick wins without some of the organisational features being in place that are required for success. For example, we have seen cases where the school had already planned its staff meetings for the year and was unable to switch these to using them in a more strategic way in the first year. Given the lack of meeting time, they "didn't have the time" to examine the data and follow through on the cycles. We have also seen schools that needed a new school year to put in place new positions to help drive the cycles. One school used a vacancy to create a new role where a teacher with some data literacy and leadership ability could lead the improvement cycle work. In the first year they were missing an enthusiast to really drive the process. Thus, the first year of implementing this approach is often a year of learning about what is needed in the organisational conditions to make the process work efficiently in the second year and beyond. The second year is usually when most schools that truly adopt this approach see big shifts in their lag data because they have the systems in place and people driving processes.

A school that has conscientiously pursued quick wins and tracked their impact during the year should see the lift in their lag data. When graphing the data and presenting it to staff, it is time to celebrate. It is easy to forget to stop and really celebrate one's success, but it is important to do so. Teachers need to be thanked for their efforts to turn results around. Then it is time to consider what has been learnt from this effort and what must be done to maintain or build on these results. This usually means returning to the fishbone diagram to re-examine the theory for improvement. Thus, practices and strategies are altered and another cycle begins. It is then important to ensure that the improvement already achieved is sustained.

Sustaining improvement should not be an issue, because the improvement cycle process should have resulted in a method of monitoring results in an ongoing and timely way. For example, after one school had lifted its written language results to the desired level, they put in place a routine to sustain those improvements. In their case, the leadership team collected a student sample of written language twice a year, analysed and graphed results, and reported back to staff on any trends that might be troublesome, such as a slip in basic skills.

Another method of sustaining improvement is to take a *major/minor* focus approach. In the written language example, once the written language target was met, it became the school's minor focus for the year, and they revisited it in at least one staff meeting per term, while most of the staff meetings would focus on the major focus, or new goal. In this way, every year there is a clear major goal focus, but the last area of improvement (the minor focus) is also closely monitored and revisited with professional learning as required. The key to success is the systems that are built into the new ways of working.

Thus, what is learnt in one year is not dropped and forgotten when a new focus is engaged with.

Key Points

- Checking and refining occurs at two levels. First, lead indicators, the quick-win data of student outcomes and the process data that inform the leadership team whether, or to what extent, teachers have implemented the agreed changes, are reviewed, and strategies and measurement tools are refined in the next cycle in response to it. Second, the lag indicators, which usually draw on external qualification data or standardised tests, are reviewed annually, and goals and targets are re-set.
- For ease of ongoing analysis, schools should keep their own version of their lag data in a *data overview* document that they add to each year.
- If quick-win data do not show improvement, schools need to review their theory for improvement and their measurement tool to identify reasons. Refinements are made in the next cycle according to the theory they develop.
- Sometimes schools do not get a big lift in their lag data in their first year of using improvement cycles, often because they have not had the organisational practices in place to support the process. These problems can usually be addressed between academic years.
- Qualitative data are also important to collect and review, such as any reactions from students, teachers, and leaders to the processes or tools and their perceptions of the impact.

References

Highfield, C. (2010). Disparity in student achievement within and across secondary schools: An analysis of department results in English, maths and science in New Zealand. *School Leadership and Management, 30*(2), 171–190.

Hinnant-Crawford, B. N. (2020). *Improvement science in education: A primer*. Myers Education Press.

CHAPTER ELEVEN

Leading Improvement—The Human Side of Change

This book has focused on the technical side of making changes to achieve an improvement in student outcomes, but it has not yet addressed the human side of leading staff to improve outcomes. There is no doubt that leading change in the way a school operates can be a testing time for a leadership team and for staff. Leadership, however, demands that improvement is sought. Without that goal focus, there is no leadership. This chapter outlines some of the skills required for successful leadership of improvement cycles in relation to the human side of change. We highlight how leaders can attract people to the change and motivate engagement, and we address the issues that all leaders face at some point, such as negativity and resistance from staff.

Attracting People to the Change

To attract staff to the improvement process, there are a number of strategies that effective lead teams use. The first is to treat everyone's views with respect and genuinely engage with their views and beliefs, especially if these views differ from their own. We refer to this as engaging in constructive problem talk (Robinson, 2018). Second, trust is important to enable open discussions, collaborative problem-solving, and risk taking (i.e., to change practice or to try new approaches). Another strategy is to build the collective efficacy of staff by resourcing the change adequately so they experience success. When staff are involved in decision making, are trusted in their professional work, and see short-term results arising from small, agreed-upon changes in their practice, their commitment to the goal and their desire to continue to pursue it increases. They are unlikely to experience this success unless prior thought is given as to how and when teachers can meet to do this work, or how to ensure that it does not create an unreasonable burden on staff's time and energy. Next, we elaborate on these ideas.

Engage Teachers' Theories of Action

Engaging in constructive problem talk requires a person to understand the concept of a *theory of action*. Theories of action are frameworks for understanding what drives people's behaviours. Our actions or inactions are driven by our beliefs or values. These actions or inactions have consequences, some of which are intended and some of which are not. Our beliefs and values, our actions and inactions, and the consequences of those, form our theories of action. A theory of action makes the linkage between these aspects explicit. For example, a leader's belief that the school cannot improve a certain problematic result may be due to the fact that they have had that level of performance for many years. They believe that the teachers work hard, but not all students are capable of learning at higher levels. These beliefs drive their actions. As a result, they design programmes to meet students' current abilities and to help them find success (their actions) rather than challenging and stretching students in their learning and risking failure (their inactions). The intended consequence of the leader's actions and inactions are that students enjoy school and feel successful, but the unintended consequence is that students might not reach their full potential, and their options beyond school may be limited by their lack of qualifications (see, for example, Wilson et al., 2016).

People hold beliefs about what the problem is, what the causes of a problem are, and what likely solutions are. Engaging constructively with each others' theories of action around a problem is not always easy, as even the word "problem" is not part of the lexicon of some school leaders. However, both problem avoidance and "blaming problem talk" are ineffective in engaging others in improvement efforts (Robinson, 2018, p. 41). This means that all parties need to be able to express their beliefs about problems, and the grounds for them.

Challenging others' beliefs can often result in defensiveness, especially if challenging these beliefs involves a critique of other peoples' actions. For example, if teachers are being challenged in their belief that students' current achievement levels are satisfactory and that they have done all they could to improve, they are likely to defend their belief, because anything else is an admission of failure on their part for past actions. This reaction is entirely understandable and something we all engage in at times. This *defensive reasoning* (Argyris, 1991) results from being put in an uncomfortable position because our long-held theory of action is being questioned. We can all help others to move beyond defensive reasoning by truly engaging with their theory of action, rather than bypassing it (Robinson, 2018).

Bypassing a theory of action involves ignoring people's beliefs that drive their current actions and trying to persuade them of a better way of doing things. Engaging with their theory of action means working hard to truly understand what people's beliefs *are* before advocating for any variation on that belief system. This involves the interpersonal leadership skills outlined above, which include open disclosure of one's own beliefs and genuine inquiry into others' beliefs and reasoning. As Robinson (2018) says, "engagement requires both parties to have access to each other's thinking" (p. 60).

For example, in a secondary school where the leadership team identified external examination results as unsatisfactory and drew the conclusion that poor levels of literacy were undermining students' ability to thrive, middle leaders were quick to point to a number of reasons. First, they argued, they were not teachers of literacy. Second, literacy should have been taught in primary school. Third, they did not have time to teach literacy skills, nor did they have the expertise to do so. These beliefs would drive the extent to which these middle leaders encouraged their teams to include a focus on literacy in their planning. To engage with these beliefs, a leader would acknowledge the correctness of these points. For example, students should have learnt these skills in primary school. Unfortunately, they did not. They

would agree that secondary school teachers were there for their subject expertise and that they did not have depth of knowledge in literacy. They could also agree that teachers are time-poor already and
struggle to teach the existing course content. By summarising these
views and not arguing with them (because they are essentially correct), the leader would be showing that they have heard and understood the middle leaders' points of view. If there are beliefs that need to
be challenged, then they need to be challenged in a respectful manner.

A starting point for improvement is the agreement on a problem—
here leaders can note that there was agreement that literacy results
were problematic. A discussion could evolve around the importance of
the problem and reason to engage in solving it—for example, evidence
that students' lack of literacy skills was a hindering factor for students
achieving qualifications across different departments. Highlighting
the importance of the problem and its impact will increase commitment to the problem-solving process.

Then beliefs about the causes and potential solutions can be further unpacked. For example, staff could agree that the school had no
control over what was or was not taught in primary school; thus the
school cannot address this aspect. Teachers could be engaged in a collaborative, problem-solving discussion about small changes in practice that could build literacy skills across the school with a literacy
expert's help. Such changes might comprise a change in pedagogical
approach, but one that does not impact teaching time or require a
high level of preparation by subject teachers. For example, one potential strategy might be for all teachers to agree to move away from
providing students with summaries of key facts, and instead provide
them once a fortnight with a short, one- or two-paragraph piece of
adult-level text (e.g., from a newspaper article) that students must
read and elicit the main points. This exercise can be carried out in
any subject, and leaders could model the approach to the teachers. In
this way, middle leaders' or teachers' theories on the problem are not
ignored, but an alternative theory is developed.

Engaging with teachers' theories of action does not mean a ready
acceptance or agreement with their beliefs and reasoning, but an
open discussion about beliefs and reasoning. When focused on school

improvement, it is critical that the lead team keeps the focus on the "student-centred" problem and that data are always used to illustrate the problem. Comparing the school's performance to similar schools' better performance, or their own school's declining improvement over time, is often the means for doing this. While gaining agreement that results could be improved, the difficulties often lie in discussing the reasons for low results or a lack of improvement. It is here, as in the example just cited, that external factors are often pointed out—for instance, the nature of the school community or other reasons outside the school's control. It is critical that the lead team is upfront and unequivocable when they see results as unsatisfactory and that they lead teachers to focus on what can be done to foster improvement.

Build Trust

Effective leadership focuses on improvement and problem-solving in a way that promotes collective trust. When there is trust, people are willing to make themselves vulnerable and take risks, because they trust others to be understanding if there is an unintentional slip-up. This trust makes a team efficient because everyone can get on with the job and rely on each other for suppport. They do not have to constantly get permission to progress their work, and they know they can try new approaches and practices. Risk-taking is encouraged rather than penalised. Trust also builds internal commitment to the improvement work, as staff feel they are pulling in the same direction. Teachers in high-trust schools go the extra mile, engage more readily in change, and achieve higher outcomes for students (Bryk & Schneider, 2002).

A more productive and trusting culture is developed when leaders act in respectful, well-intentioned, and competent ways, are transparent with information, share the decsion-making process, and show integrity in the implementation of agreed actions. First, leaders need to recognise that each staff member is an important part of the school and show their respect and interest in supporting them. Trust is built through interactions with others, and thus leaders engaging with staff and enabling staff across the school to engage in collaborative problem solving and learning are important mechansims for building a trusting school culture. It is in these interactions that people judge competence, integrity, genuine interest, and trustworthiness. Leaders thus need to find opportunities to engage with their staff across the school, rather than only lead from behind their office door or through the proxy of the team around them.

Second, transparency and shared decision making evolves from engaging with teachers' theories of actions and clearly communicating the reasoning behind decisions teachers or groups of staff were not involved in. When teachers are part of the decision making, they are more likely to embrace the changes. That is why formally using an improvement cycle approach faciliates a positive culture of professionalism and success. The formally developed theory for improvement is communicated and provides signposts on practices and expectations. This working theory develops over time, and changes are communicated by the active involvement of teachers in problem-solving in each subsequent cycle. Furthermore, changes to practice are first being *tested* to see if they bring improvement. Thus, teachers can trust that they are not thrown into the dark to test things, but that these changes have already been tested in a couple of classrooms. Finally, standard work processes and practical measures that offer coherence across the school are implemented. The protocols that are developed for data collection and reporting are designed not to be burdensome, but to link into teachers' daily work. It makes the work of improvement business-as-usual and builds trust—because all are involved, and processes are efficient and transparent.

Finally, trust is based on the expectations we have of others. Often trust is lost when there is a misalignment or misunderstanding about what roles and responsibilities others have. Leaders can support the development of trust in their school by creating clarity around staff members' roles and responsibilities, and the expectations the school holds for everyone for their work and behaviour. The same is true for relationships with students and families: the expectations, roles, and responsibilities of each party need to be agreed upon to create the basis for trusting relationships.

Build Collective Efficacy

In the example provided for a theory of action, the first pedagogical quick win was small and easy to implement: "Ask students to elicit the main points from a text themselves rather than telling them; do it once in the next two weeks and then report back and discuss in the next staff meeting". This action passes the test for a good, quick win: "Is that all? I can do that." If middle leaders can see the value in a strategy, then they will encourage their teachers to engage in it, because they see the benefit for both the students and for their departments' or teams' results. When teachers see quick and worthwhile results, their confidence and that of their students grows. Self-belief and energy are driven up, and so are results. Too often, the barrier to leading improvement is that the perceived changes are seen as large and burdensome on teachers, so they do not get traction, whereas with the improvement cycle approach, groups of teachers receive concrete feedback regularly by way of students' quick-win results, which builds their belief in their power to make a difference. The efficacy of both teachers and students is a powerful factor influencing student achievement (Goddard et al., 2015), and it is built from the ongoing feedback that working through improvement cycles provides. The self-belief from seeing quick wins strengthens the goal focus and inspires more effort and persistence on the part of both students and teachers. Over time, the collective efficacy of staff at the school will build. This collective feeling of everyone pulling together and being able to make a difference will increase motivation for change across the school.

Resource the Change

The lead team's role is to set the conditions for a cycle of improvement to occur without being a burden on teachers, or as a way of shaming or belittling teachers. When well implemented, improvement cycles help teachers and students see visible improvement, and support teachers to learn on the job in an authentic, systematic way. Leaders need to think about where resourcing is most needed and

how to support teachers' learning in a strategic way. Support can take
the form of specific professional learning in relation to the problem
and the goal being addressed. It can also be provided by building leadership capabilities. However, resourcing to enable collaborative problem-solving and learning on the basis of quick wins is the key to building a sustainable approach to implementing improvement cycles.
This requires that leaders think about staff's roles and responsibilities and their meeting structures, and are prepared to make adjustments to them.

Changing and resourcing a different meeting structure to create the condition of improvement was illustrated in Chapter Two,
when the lead team of Gauguin Primary set up pods of about three
teachers working at the same level. The school facilitated their joint
release during class time to examine and act on quick-win data. While
teacher release comes with high costs, the school placed the priority
on collaborative problem solving and optimising teachers' ability to
engage with the quick-win data; it was the lead team's role to find the
resources.

However, it is not enough to give teachers the time. That time
must be used well, and that means a member of the lead team or a
middle leader needs to be in the meetings to guide teachers, at least
initially. Protocols for running the meetings and reporting quick-win
results need to be established along with a timeline, and leaders must
be prepared to challenge teachers' beliefs, when needed, or to offer
support. Support and challenge are both required. This is why early
investment in the middle leaders' skills and their commitment to the
process are so critical. Their leadership is required to get the process
working as a regular and effective routine for improving teaching and
learning.

Dealing With Resistance

Regardless of the skill of the principal and lead team, resistance is
common. Sometimes it is made evident in passive–aggressive ways,
such as the use of negative body language or talking negatively with

other staff in the carpark or, at other times, there is open and disrespectful challenge to leaders from staff. It is helpful for leaders to reframe their understanding of behaviour that they interpret as resistance and, instead, seek to understand the underlying beliefs that drive the behaviour.

Understand Resistance as Reaction to Risk

Teachers' apparent opposition to leadership initiatives can be understood by viewing it through the lens of *risk*. One study (Twyford et al., 2017), based on interviews of staff in three schools, demonstrated that most of the teachers perceived some risk in participating in new professional learning. Some had misgivings before experiencing the new professional learning based on past experiences, others worried about additional workload, and some worried about being shown up as inadequate in front of an expert who would observe them. These fears are quite rational and based on teachers' experience. Teachers who are new to the profession may feel less risk, as everyone acknowledges that they are newcomers and have much to learn. However, teachers who have been teaching for many years may feel a greater sense of vulnerability, as they might be expected to have a high level of expertise, given their years of service. Resistance, therefore, can be a result of fear: fear of being shown up; fear of having their time wasted because they do not believe that the new approach has merit; or fear of not being able to master a new approach. Encouraging teachers to talk about their concerns and responding to those reservations is how leaders engage teachers' theories of actions, as described earlier. Bypassing or ignoring them and hoping teachers will come around merely encourages "carpark talk" and defensiveness. The critical leadership role is to help teachers to bring any reservations to the surface so they can be addressed. This might be done early in the process by leaders being clear: "This is the problem, this is the goal, here are our initial thoughts about the first quick wins, but things can go wrong. Let's discuss that so we can mitigate any obvious risks to this plan". Lencioni (2005) would call this approach "mining for conflict". Leaders move towards conflict, surface it, and provide the space to consider different concerns from the team. Too often conflict is avoided and then starts to simmer below the surface. Openness to discussing and addressing concerns means that when the team moves to make a final decision about what they will pursue and how, teachers are more likely to feel committed.

Expect Some Attrition

There needs to be some pragmatism, as often not all staff will "get on board". It is unrealistic to seek 100% agreement from staff. They might believe in a different approach or be too set in their ways. Further, sometimes changes need to be made whether they are initially popular with teachers or not. If a school is underperforming, urgent action is required. Principals of schools that improve have high expectations for staff and students and often bring in changes quickly as they determine that another cohort of students can wait no longer. If there is not an acceptable status quo in the school, and the students suffer from lack of standards and coherence across the school, principals need to act. There are bottom lines in all workplaces, and schools should not be an exception. It is reasonable to expect all teachers to meet deadlines and to have a certain level of expertise in their job. Once a goal is decided on and a strategy has been tested and shown to work, all teachers should be expected to engage. Teachers have to be part of a team focused on purposeful improvement if a school is to turn around results. When principals and senior leaders have this unrelenting focus on gaining improvement, it will not be comfortable for every teacher, which is why improving schools—particularly larger schools—tend to have more staff turnover than schools that are already high-performing (Bendikson, 2012; Chenoweth, 2007). In high-performing schools, the norms involved in attaining and maintaining those standards have been set over time. But when a school is relatively low-performing, and it starts on an improvement trajectory, the new norms need to be established (Schein, 2004). Some staff inevitably decide they might prefer to work elsewhere. The turnover of staff who do not want to work in a more visible, results-oriented, and collaborative way present an opportunity for senior leaders to employ new staff with a commitment to high standards. These new appointments are one of the ways that school cultures are incrementally influenced, along with clear expectations, transparent roles and responsibilities, coherent routines and practices, and leaders role-modelling the way they approach problems.

People who undermine those efforts (either covertly or overtly) need to have their voices heard, but bad behaviour should not be tolerated. Too often in schools, leaders turn the other way instead of confronting unacceptable behaviour or unacceptable results (Mintrop & Zumpe, 2019; Patuawa et al., 2021). Ignoring poor adult behaviour or poor results is a failure of leadership, and it is read that way by the other staff, who work hard to do the right thing by their students and their colleagues. Bypassing bad behaviour—for example, "failure to attend meetings, frequent interruptions, personally hostile attacks, and the like" (Schein, 2004, p. 74)—will only result in lack of trust in the leadership. Leaders show competence by addressing poor behaviour: "The standard you walk past is the standard you accept" (Lieutenant-General David Morrison; Chief of Army, Australia; 2016 Australian of the Year).

Conclusion

In conclusion, while this book is entitled "It's not rocket science", leading improvement is challenging, particularly as teams learn the process and develop a new culture within their schools. New habits and expectations lead to a new sense of *normal*, one where there is a heightened sense of accountability for the results of every student. The School Improvement Cycle becomes less visible as it is enacted routinely through new "working procedures, measurements, and rules of interaction" (Schein, 2004, p. 67). Rockets do not crash to the ground, and astronauts do not die in schools if results do not improve, or if they regress. But leaders who implement improvement cycles feel just as much anxiety as they await the results of their lag data as the rocket scientists feel as they await the safe return of their rockets. It is the test of their collective effectiveness. They have a major stake in it. Pursuing school improvement is not rocket science, but it is a science: improvement science. And all the small tests and small, yet highly visible, quick wins they make through the year provide the confidence that their "school rocket" will safely land.

Key Points

- Attract staff to the change by engaging with their theories of actions, resourcing the change adequately, and ensuring that what is asked of teachers is not burdensome.
- Resistance should be understood as a response to risk. Engage with those feelings openly to build trust.

References

Argyris, C. (1991). Teaching smart people how to learn. *Harvard Business Review*, May–June, 5–15.

Bendikson, L. (2012). *The effects of principal instructional leadership on secondary school performance*. The University of Auckland.

Bryk, A. S., & Schneider, B. (2002). *Trust in schools: A core resource for improvement*. Russell Sage Foundation.

Chenoweth, K. (2007). *It's being done: Academic success in unexpected schools*. Harvard Education Press.

Goddard, R., Goddard, Y., Kim, E. S., & Miller, R. (2015). A theoretical and empirical analysis of the roles of instructional leadership, teacher collaboration, and collective efficacy beliefs in support of student learning. *American Journal of Education, 121*, 501–528.

Lencioni, P. (2005). *Overcoming the five dysfunctions of a team: A field guide*. Jossey-Bass.

Mintrop, R., & Zumpe, E. (2019). Solving real-life problems of practice and education leaders' school improvement mind-set. *American Journal of Education, 125*, 295–344.

Patuawa, J., Robinson, V. M. J., Sinnema, C., & Zhu, T. (2021). Addressing inequity and underachievement: Middle leaders' effectiveness in problem solving. *Leading and Managing, 27*(1), 51–78.

Robinson, V. M. J. (2018). *Reduce change to increase improvement*. Corwin.

Schein, E. H. (2004). *Organizational culture and leadership* (3rd ed.). Jossey-Bass.

Twyford, K., Le Fevre, D., & Timperley, H. (2017). The influence of risk and uncertainty on teachers' responses to professional learning and development. *Journal of Professional Capital and Community, 2*(2), 86–100. https://doi.org/10.1108/JPCC-10-2016-0028

Wilson, A., Madjar, I., & McNaughton, S. (2016). Opportunity to learn about disciplinary literacy in senior secondary English classrooms in New Zealand. *The Curriculum Journal, 27*(2), 204–228. https://doi.org/10.1080/09585176.2015.1134339

ABOUT THE AUTHORS

Dr Linda Bendikson

Linda has been involved in educational leadership in New Zealand her whole career: as a principal of a two-teacher school serving a rural Māori community, as an adviser to rural schools, as a deputy principal, and then as the principal of a provincial city school in the 1990s. She went on to become a regional manager in the Ministry of Education of New Zealand for 10 years whilst completing a PhD on "The Effects of Principal Instructional Leadership on Secondary School Performance" under the supervision of Professors Viviane Robinson and John Hattie at the University of Auckland. Linda then worked for the University of Auckland and spent eight years leading the Centre for Educational Leadership before heading into private consultancy work in 2019. Her schooling improvement and leadership development programs (*Leading Teams* and *Leading Improvement*) are delivered online to New Zealand and Australian schools. Her programs support teams of leaders to do the real work of improvement. She guides leadership teams through the process of implementing improvement cycles and effectively leading change. She has been actively involved in researching school improvement and leadership since completing her PhD, frequently publishing with Dr Frauke Meyer.

Linda is a pragmatist who draws on her practical experience and her academic interests in goal theory and improvement science to support school leaders to carry out their roles more strategically and effectively. As someone who never had the benefit of leadership training until very late in her career, her mission is to improve learners' outcomes by increasing the efficiency and effectiveness of leaders in schools and schooling systems.

Dr Frauke Meyer

Frauke is a senior lecturer in the Faculty of Education and Social Work at the University of Auckland. She teaches and supervises students in the Master of Educational Leadership program. Frauke trained as a teacher for students with special needs in Germany, completing a master's degree in teaching and working across schools to support their inclusion efforts. She moved to New Zealand in 2008 and completed another master's degree and a PhD under the supervision of Professor Stuart McNaughton. Whilst working on her PhD, Frauke worked for several research projects of small to large scale in New Zealand and Australia, including as a researcher for the Centre for Educational Leadership (UACEL). She continued her work for the centre, mainly supporting the First-time Principals' Programme, and worked closely with Distinguished Professor Viviane Robinson during these years before taking up a lecturer position at the faculty.

Frauke's research is concerned with school improvement, school leadership, and interpersonal leadership practices. The immediate focus of her research is leadership practices that foster school improvement and create equity in outcomes. In her research, she works closely with schools and school leaders in prioritising outcomes for schools. Linda and Frauke have worked closely at the Centre for Educational Leadership on research projects focussed on school improvement projects, and in teaching at the faculty and in professional development courses. Frauke has presented and published her research internationally at conferences and in high-quality journals. Her aim is to support schools and leaders in improving equity in outcomes for their learners through effective and strategic system leadership.

INDEX